HEALTH TOURISM

HEALTH TOURISM

By

R. Thompson

DISCOVERY PUBLISHING HOUSE PVT. LTD.

NEW DELHI-110 002

Published by:
Tilak Wasan
DISCOVERY PUBLISHING HOUSE PVT. LTD.
4383/4B, Ansari Road, Darya Ganj
New Delhi-110 002 (India)
Phone : +91-11-23279245, 43596064-65
Fax : +91-11-23253475
E-mail : discoverypublishinghouse@gmail.com
namitwasan9@gmail.com
sales@discoverypublishinggroup.com
web : www.discoverypublishinggroup.com

***First Edition:* 2011**
***Reprinted:* 2016**

ISBN: 978-81-8356-937-8

Health Tourism

Printed at:
Infinity Imaging Systems
Delhi

PREFACE

Health tourists rate safety as their number one concern when choosing their holiday destination according to new data released today by the FIA on World Tourism Day. Lack of safety whether due to crime, the risk of natural disasters, sanitary risks or terrorism, was the principle reason to rule out a destination, and scored highest in the survey with 8.5 points out of a possible 10. Safety was closely followed by weather which received an average 8.2 points, quality of accommodation received 8.2 points, and natural beauty 8.0 points.

Health care is the treatment and prevention of illness. Health care is delivered by professionals in medicine, dentistry, nursing, pharmacy and allied health. Thailand looks back upon a rich traditional and natural alternative medical history containing the famous Thai massage and the well-known Thai wellness spa therapy. Complementing these physical treatments, Thailand banks on a very special cuisine, made of fresh vegetables, fruits, herbs, which when cooked carefully with fish, is the basis for many detoxification, weight loss, rejuvenation methods for people who wish to refresh and re-energise from a hectic lifestyle.

The World Health Organization (WHO) is a specialized United Nations agency which acts as a coordinator and researcher for public health around the world. Health economics is a branch of economics concerned with issues related to scarcity in the allocation of health and health care. Broadly, health economists study the functioning of the health care system and the private and social causes of health-affecting behaviors such as smoking.

Health system reform in the United States usually focuses around three suggested systems, with proposals currently underway to integrate these systems in various ways to provide a number of health care options. First is single-payer, a term meant to describe a single agency managing a single system, as found in most modernized countries as well as some states and municipalities within the United States. Second are employer or individual insurance mandates, with which the state of Massachusetts has experimented.

While compiling research material for this book, we surf many websites, visit many libraries for ensuring the authenticity of the matter and current updates. We are sincerely grateful to all these resources as without this the publication of this book wouldn't have been possible. Our main aim is to spread the light of knowledge to the readers, so that the darkness of ignorance dispels away.

—Author

CONTENTS

1

INTRODUCTION

Health tourism is also called medical travel, medical tourism or global healthcare. It is a term initially coined by travel agencies and the mass media to describe the rapidly-growing practice of travelling across international borders to obtain health care. It also refers pejoratively to the practice of healthcare providers travelling internationally to deliver healthcare.

India's health tourism sector is expected to experience an annual growth rate of 30%, making it a Rs. 9,500-crore industry by 2015. Estimates of the value of medical tourism to India go as high as $2 billion a year by 2012. Advantages for health tourists include reduced costs, the availability of latest medical technologies and a growing compliance on international quality standards, as well as the fact that foreigners are not likely to face a language barrier in India. The Indian government is taking steps to address infrastructure issues that hinder the country's growth in health tourism.

The social and political issues surrounding access to health care in the US have led to vigorous public debate and the almost colloquial use of terms such as health care (medical management of illness), health insurance (reimbursement of health care costs), and public health (the collective state and range of health in a population). The delivery of modern health care depends on an expanding group of trained professionals coming together as an interdisciplinary team.

HEALTH CARE AND HEALTH TOURISM

The health-care industry incorporates several sectors that are dedicated to providing health care services and products. According to industry and market classifications, such as the Global Industry Classification Standard and the Industry Classification Benchmark, the health-care industry includes health care equipment and services as well as pharmaceuticals, biotechnology and life sciences. The particular sectors associated with these groups are: biotechnology, diagnostic substances, drug delivery, drug manufacturers, hospitals, medical equipment and instruments, diagnostic laboratories, nursing homes, providers of health care plans and home health care.

Health care is the treatment and prevention of illness. Health care is delivered by professionals in medicine, dentistry, nursing, pharmacy and allied health.India has all the ingredients to develop into a sophisticated medical tourism destination. It has a long-standing traditional herbal and alternative treatments history, it has various weather zones to cater for different types of stay, people speak English, its academics and physicians are sophisticated and knowledgeable. What is needed now is the upgrading of infrastructure and facilities.

Kerala, the name almost synonymous with the word 'Ayurveda', is now all set to reap the benefits of Ayurveda through health tourism. The reason for this is the popularity of Ayurvedic treatments and the manner in which Kerala is marketing Ayurveda in medical tourism. In the 1950s, Kerala had a State Hospitality Department.

However, the functions of the department were confined to running of guest house, upkeep of residential bungalows of ministers and providng hospitality and other arrangements of VVIPs. At that time, there were not many hotels where foreign tourists could stay. Hence, they used to get accommodation in government guest house. "But, in the 1960s, the traffic of tourists started to increase.

Thailand looks back upon a rich traditional and natural alternative medical history containing the famous Thai massage and the well-known Thai wellness spa therapy. Complementing these physical treatments, Thailand banks on a very special cuisine, made of fresh vegetables, fruits, herbs, which when cooked carefully with fish, is the basis for many detoxification, weight loss, rejuvenation methods for people who wish to refresh and re-energise from a hectic lifestyle.

All these are part of the complementary medical treatments available alongside the numerous state-of-the-art hospitals in Bangkok and the major cities of the country, which were developed over the past 5-6 years. These hospitals now termed as 'international' have upgraded their facilities and personnel to cater to the needs and expectations of demanding international visitors. They offer special reception facilities with multilingual staff, swift and sophisticated referral procedures, leading edge diagnostic technology paired with experienced and knowledgeable physicians who have gained practical experience abroad. The range of treatments in the hospitals covers different parts of the body, from top to toe, and the prices are very reasonable for people coming from the dollar/euro/pound zones.

People who travel with the purpose of purchasing medical and wellness treatments alongside any other desired infrastructural services (logistics, attractions) are defined as medical tourists, and belong to the special interest segments of general tourism. Hospitals, besides having to offer specialised medical interventions, have become part of overall travel-services packages. Although the major point of interest for a medical tourist is taking care of his health conditions, complementary services like airport welcome, transportation, accommodation, escort and translations, accounting-audits are also booked and assembled into a services package.

Accompanying persons (family, partners or friends) need attention while their companions are being treated. To complete the whole picture, rehabilitation treatment is usually provided in specialised health resorts, mostly outside of towns. Besides, specialised packages in rehabilitation, prevention, rejuvenation, re-energising mostly sought after by Europeans seeking holistic treatment vacations should also be considered part of the larger healthcare tourism. These are booked as typical (however, specialised) vacation packages.

It was then the government realised that there is a lot of potential in the hotel sector. So, a separate Department of Tourism came into being. Soon Kerala realised that it had a huge market for health tourism. Tourists would automatically be inclined towards Ayurveda. It was a natural attraction; the credit goes to the positive results on health improvement and no side effects of Ayurveda.

The promotion of Ayurveda in health tourism started in 1994 and the Kerala Tourism Development Corporation (KTDC) started Ayurvedic health centres in its premium properties like Hotel Samudra, Kovalam during the same period. "KTDC has tied up with the most reputed Ayurveda treatment providers and hence the authority of doctors and the quality of the medicines used are not compromised. The response has been encouraging," says Raj Mohan, Marketing Manager, KTDC.

Besides India, the countries inclined towards Ayurveda are UK, France, Spain, Italy and also some Gulf countries like Saudi Arabia and the UAE. However, the award for the most number of tourists coming to India is bagged by Germany. And the growth rate of the tourists flocking for

Ayurveda is increasing at the rate of around 20-25 per cent per annum.

Ayurvedic Resort

KTDC has recently opened up an Ayurvedic resort called 'Thanneermukkom Ayurvedic Lake Resort' located beside the pristine backwater at Thannermukkom. "Here, we have tied up with the Keraleeya Ayurveda Samajam, a society formed by the Maharaja of Zamorine of Calicut in 1903 to promote and protect Ayurveda, headed by Padmasree Dr Rajagopal. Unlike the usual Ayurvedic spa/centres attached to a hotel, this resort combines authentic Ayurvedic treatment with leisure," adds Raj.

The patient's medical records are thoroughly examined by a panel of expert doctors and treatment is suggested after verifying the medical conditions. Thus, the unique feature of the resort is that it provides treatment just like a fully-equipped Ayurveda hospital without reducing the leisure element by way of location, property etc.

Advantage Kerala

Kerala has the advantages of recognition worldwide as one of the ten must-see destinations, as described by the National Geographic Traveller and a developed healthcare delivery system, which enables the state to attract patients from other countries.

KTDC has tied-up with the Cochin-based Amrita Institute of Medical Sciences (AIMS) too, the obvious reason is that AIMS has been receiving patients from 16 countries, including European countries, and recently there is a steady increase in the number of patients coming down for Ayurveda. Through the joint venture it will be possible to offer the patients quality medical care at AIMS and tourism options for both the patients and bystanders through KTDC.

"We have a tie-up with a Korean University. It's a exchange programme, through which the university will promote our brand and in turn we will market their various study programmes," says Sree Kumar, Marketing Manager, Vaidyaratnam Nursing Home. Vaidyaratnam has more than 1,000 branches all over India, from which 20 are in Kerala, with a 35-bed facility (30 rooms and 5 cottages) each.

Kerala has recently won the Best State Award for tourism promotion from the Government of India. When asked about the role of Ayurveda in this, Suman answers diplomatically, "Kerala tourism basically revolves around four things - beaches, back waters, hill stations and Ayurveda. So, giving credit to only Ayurveda will not be fair. It has contributed as much as the other factors."

Classification of Centres

The Department of Tourism has classified all the Ayurvedic centres in two categories-Green Leaf and Olive Leaf. The department does not take responsibility of any centre which is not classified in either of the above. "The most difficult part is letting the tourists know about this classification. I make sure to stress this particular point whenever I am in any travel mart abroad," says Suman, who adds that almost five lakh foreign tourists come to Kerala annually for Ayurvedic treatments.

Marketing Strategies

Kerala recently participated in the Information Technology Business (ITB), 2006. Every year, there are some new additions to promote Ayurveda. This year, it was Ayurveda Masseur, where a quick Ayurvedic massage was given to foreigners, "To give them a taste of what exactly is Ayurveda and how wondrous it can be. And if they want more, they can always visit Kerala for it," avers Suman.

Apart from the masseurs, Kerala is always organising road shows all around the world for the promotion of Ayurveda along with modern medicine. The latest one being at France, others at Berlin and London. They will continue with the road shows in the future also.

It is not a compulsion for the tourists to avail the other two facilities, if they do not want to," says Geeta. She does not forget to add that 90 per cent of the tourists visiting her resorts are from abroad, as Indians are not too much interested in the Ayurvedic treatments. When asked about how many of the total visitors at Kairali Resorts come exclusively for Ayurveda, she promptly replies, "All of them".

Vegetarian Food

In Ayurveda, food is given utmost importance. "We serve only vegetarian food while the tourists are undergoing Ayurvedic treatments for arthritis and paralysis." Also, the contents of the meal differ from person to person depending on the kind of problems they are facing. "Protein-rich food is given at our hospital and we also serve non-vegetarian food, but only grilled or baked," adds Dr Mohan Babu, Chief of Staff, Krishnendu Ayurvedic Hospital, a chain of two 40-bed hospitals.

With so many Ayurvedic hospitals all over Kerala, there is a possibility that the tourists will choose them over resorts. But Geeta says, "In resorts, tourists can just stay for a few hours, get treated and go enjoy their holidays. But in the hospitals, people feel like they are really very sick and they cannot move around freely. Even the atmosphere at the resorts is more relaxing and that helps in quick recovery."

But there is another aspect to this. While and after undergoing Ayurvedic medical treatment, one is supposed to take complete rest. "The tourists here come, take treatment and then they want to go swimming and running on the beach. We do not allow this," avers Dr Mohan, who receives almost 70 outpatients on a daily basis. And the treatment days can range from seven days to 21 days, depending on the problem the patient is facing.

"Some tourists ask for chicken all the time, but we are very srtict", says Dr PK Lathika, Chief Physician, Sarathy Ayrvedic Hospital, a 30-bed hospital in Elookkara, Kerala. With the importance of accreditation of the Ayurvedic centres, every resort and hospital is looking forward to a government accreditation. And Geeta is very proud to say, "Along with the accreditation of our resort in Kerala, the Ministry was quite happy with the kind of quality offered at Kairali. The Ministry of Tourism even complimented our group saying - Your organisation will act as a role model for all the other Ayurvedic centres."

Obstacles

"Travel agents stress only on the massage part of Ayurveda. The pleasure part is given utmost importance in their agenda. They must also make people understand that Ayurveda cures many complex problems, like paralysis, which they will get only at an Ayurvedic hospital, under the observation of qualified doctors," says Dr Babu.

There are a lot of illegal activities going on in the name of Ayurveda. As a result, it proves very challenging to convince tourists and Indian citizens to actually come and visit the Ayurvedic centre. "Authenticity becomes suspect for the visitors. Strong monitoring is required," adds Kuroop, whose hospital was featured in one of the episodes of CNBC's Crime Watch, which dealt with the topic of the name of Ayurvedic massage parlours being used for indecent activities. The accreditation system of the tourism department is a relief to all the Ayurvedic centres.

"We face problems in exporting our medicines. Foreign countries have a compulsion of a certification regarding non-existence of metals in medicines. We have to spend almost 20 lakh for this certification", says Kumar, whose organisation manufactures 400 ayurvedic products, from the old Ayurvedic texts.

Hyderabad is fast becoming a major health tourism centre as many foreign patients are opting to get treated here. Hyderabad has become one of the major health tourism hubs in India as a number of hospitals are providing services at affordable costs. Hundreds of foreigners are showing interest to obtain better health care treatment in Hyderabad hospitals which employ the latest technology and have modern facilities.

Promotion Plans

Along with the projects already being carried on, there is always a need to make future plans for promotion. There is close competition in the Ayurvedic sector now. Existing and new hotels are compelled to have an Ayurvedic spa. In such cut throat competition, experienced and well-established hospitals also are now waking up to this. "We are planning to have a tie-up soon with the travel agents abroad. This will help us have greater exposure. Also, we will soon be having a tie-up with Yahoo and Google," adds Dr Babu. The Kairali Group has many projects lined up. The first thing they are planning is franchising. "An agreement with Vietnam is already in the pipeline. The others waiting include an agreement with Czechoslovakia and even China seems eager to sign one."

"Holding exhibitions abroad is one thing we are looking forward to," says Kuroop, who already has patients lined up from countries like the US, Germany, UK, Italy and Spain. "We are also coming up with an e-discount coupon for Hutch subscribers, wherein if the subscriber wants to avail of the discount, he can get in touch with our hospital and we will send him the discount coupon on his cell. Simultaneously, our system will be informed about it." Apart from this,

Kerala Vaidyashala will be involved in cross promotion with the Apollo group of hospitals. While the Apollo group will promote Vaidyashalas' services, they will in turn market Apollo.

"We are planning for franchisees in the Middle East, as it does not have many complications and getting an approval for business in Ayurveda is easy," adds Kumar. Vaidyaratnam is also planning additional 15 cottages at each of its centres. "We are overbooked for three months."

Promotion of Ayurveda is done in print and electronic media too. But, the travel agents abroad help in better exposure and marketing. One reason for that is, they have their own clientele and they are the ones who can influence tourists to visit a particular resort or spa. Another good option is to participate in the ITB held annually. So, when there is sévere threat from each other to all Ayurvedic hospitals and resorts, there is one Big Daddy who will benefit in any case: The Kerala Tourism Department!

Guidelines for accreditation of Ayurvedic and Panchakarma centres have been finalised and issued for implementation. It has been decided to prepare and print brochures, CDs and other publicity material to promote Ayurveda in medical tourism. Medical and health tourism has been specifically promoted at various international platforms such as World Travel Mart, London. So, the Tourism Ministry is all set to reap the benefits of Ayurveda in a huge way.

Industry Classification

According to government industry classifications, which are mostly based on the United Nations system, the International Standard Industrial Classification, health care generally consists of hospital activities, medical and dental practice activities, and other human health activities. The last class consists of all activities for human health not performed by hospitals, physicians or dentists.

This involves activities of, or under the supervision of, nurses, midwives, physiotherapists, scientific or diagnostic laboratories, pathology clinics, home, or other para-medical practitioners in the field of optometry, hydrotherapy, medical massage, yoga therapy, music therapy, occupational therapy, speech therapy, chiropody, homeopathy, chiropractics, acupuncture, etc.

The philosophy of healthcare attempts to synthesize the general meaning of the healthcare industry as a social institution. Through the study of people, processes, politics, and ethics in the healthcare industry, a workable philosophy of healthcare develops. And as a social philosophy, healthcare represents the primary means by which people improve the overall quality of their daily lives. The ultimate purpose of healthcare philosophy is to provide an analytic framework for the collection and analysis of all pertinent data in the healthcare industry, especially for fields like biotechnology, medicine, and nursing.

Medical Research and WHO

Medical research can be divided into two general categories: the evaluation of new treatments for both safety and efficacy in what are termed clinical trials, and all other research that contributes to the development of new treatments. The latter is termed preclinical research if its goal is specifically to elaborate knowledge for the development of new therapeutic strategies. A new paradigm to biomedical research is being termed translational research, which focuses on iterative feedback loops between the basic and clinical research domains to accelerate knowledge translation from the bedside to the bench, and back again.

In terms of pharmaceutical R&D spending, Europe spends a little less than the United States (€22.50bn compared to €27.05bn in 2006) and there is less growth in European R&D spending. Pharmaceuticals and other medical devices are the leading high technology exports of Europe and the United States. However, the United States dominates the biopharmaceutical field, accounting for the three quarters of the world's biotechnology revenues and 80% of world R&D spending in biotechnology.

The World Health Organization (WHO) is a specialized United Nations agency which acts as a coordinator and researcher for public health around the world. Established on 7 April 1948, and headquartered in Geneva, Switzerland, the agency inherited the mandate and resources of its predecessor, the Health Organization, which had been an agency of the League of Nations. The WHO's constitution states that its mission "is the attainment by all peoples of the highest possible level of health."

Its major task is to combat disease, especially key infectious diseases, and to promote the general health of the peoples of the world. Examples of its work include years of fighting smallpox. In 1979 the WHO declared that the disease had been eradicated - the first disease in history to be completely eliminated by deliberate human design. The WHO is nearing success in developing vaccines against malaria and schistosomiasis and aims to eradicate polio within the next few years. The organization has already endorsed the world's first official HIV/AIDS Toolkit for Zimbabwe from October 3, 2006, making it an international standard.

The WHO is financed by contributions from member states and from donors. In recent years the WHO's work has involved more collaboration, currently around 80 such partnerships, with NGOs and the pharmaceutical industry, as well as with foundations such as the Bill and Melinda Gates Foundation and the Rockefeller Foundation. Voluntary contributions to the WHO from national and local governments, foundations and NGOs, other UN organizations, and the private sector (including pharmaceutical companies), now exceed that of assessed contributions (dues) from its 193 member nations.

Health Economists

Health economics is a branch of economics concerned with issues related to scarcity in the allocation of health and health care. Broadly, health economists study the functioning of the health care system and the private and social causes of health-affecting behaviors such as smoking.

A seminal 1963 article by Kenneth Arrow, often credited with giving rise to the health economics as a discipline, drew conceptual distinctions between health and other goals. Factors that distinguish health economics from other areas include extensive government intervention, intractable uncertainty in several dimensions, asymmetric information, and externalities. Governments tend to regulate the health care industry heavily and also tend to be the largest payer within the market. Uncertainty is intrinsic to health, both in patient outcomes and financial concerns.

The knowledge gap that exists between a physician and a patient can prevent the patient from accurately describing his symptoms or enable the physician to prescribe unnecessary but profitable services; these imbalances lead to market failures resulting from asymmetric information. Externalities arise frequently when considering health and health care, notably in the context of infectious disease. For example, making an effort to avoid catching a cold, or practicing safer sex, affects people other than the decision maker.

The scope of health economics is neatly encapsulated by Alan William's "plumbing diagram" dividing the discipline into eight distinct topics:

- What influences health? (other than health care)
- What is health and what is its value
- The demand for health care

- The supply of health care
- Micro-economic evaluation at treatment level
- Market equilibrium
- Evaluation at whole system level; and,
- Planning, budgeting and monitoring mechanisms.

Consuming just under 10 percent of gross domestic product of most developed nations, health care can form an enormous part of a country's economy. In 2008, health care consumed an average of 9.0 percent of GDP across the OECD countries with the United States (16.0%), France (11.2%), and Switzerland (10.7%)being the top three spenders.

The United States and Canada account for 48% of world pharmaceutical sales, while Europe, Japan, and all other nations account for 30%, 9%, and 13%, respectively. United States accounts for the three quarters of the world's biotechnology revenues.

SOCIAL HEALTH INSURANCE

Social health insurance is where a nation's entire population is eligible for health care coverage, and this coverage and the services provided are regulated. In almost every country, state or municipality with a government health care system a parallel private, and usually for-profit, system is allowed to operate. This is sometimes referred to as two-tier health care. The scale, extent, and funding of these private systems is variable.

A traditional view is that improvements in health result from advancements in medical science. The medical model of health focuses on the eradication of illness through diagnosis and effective treatment. In contrast, the social model of health places emphasis on changes that can be made in society and in people's own lifestyles to make the population healthier. It defines *illness* from the point of view of the individual's functioning within their society rather than by monitoring for changes in biological or physiological signs.

The United States currently operates under a mixed market health care system. Government sources (federal, state, and local) account for 45% of U.S. health care expenditures. Private sources account for the remainder of costs, with 38% of people receiving health coverage through their employers and 17% arising from other private payment such as private insurance and out-of-pocket co-pays.

Opponents of government intervention into the market generally believe that such intervention distorts pricing as government agents would be operating outside of the corporate model and the principles of market discipline; they have less short and medium-term incentives than private agents to make purchases that can generate revenues and avoid bankruptcy.

Health system reform in the United States usually focuses around three suggested systems, with proposals currently underway to integrate these systems in various ways to provide a number of health care options. First is single-payer, a term meant to describe a single agency managing a single system, as found in most modernized countries as well as some states and municipalities within the United States. Second are employer or individual insurance mandates, with which the state of Massachusetts has experimented.

Finally, there is consumer-driven health, in which systems, consumers, and patients have more control of how they access care. This is argued[by whom?] to provide a greater incentive to find cost-saving health care approaches. Critics of consumer-driven health say that it would benefit the healthy but be insufficient for the chronically sick, much as the current system operates.

Over the past thirty years, most of the nation's health care has moved from the second model operating with not-for-profit institutions to the third model operating with for-profit institutions; the greater problems with this approach have been the gradual deregulation of HMOs resulting in fewer of the promised choices for consumers, and the steady increase in consumer costs that have marginalized consumers and burdened states with excessive urgent health care costs that are avoided when consumers actually have adequate access to preventive health care.

A few states have taken serious steps toward universal health care coverage, most notably Minnesota, Massachusetts and Connecticut, with recent examples being the Massachusetts 2006 Health Reform Statute and Connecticut's SustiNet plan to provide quality, affordable health care to state residents.

CASE OF AIDS

The politics of health care depend largely on which country one is in. Current concerns in England, for instance, revolve around the use of private finance initiatives to build hospitals which it is argued costs taxpayers more in the long run. In Germany and France, concerns are more based on the rising cost of drugs to the governments. In Brazil, an important political issue is the breach of intellectual property rights, or patents, for the domestic manufacture of antiretroviral drugs used in the treatment of HIV/AIDS.

The South African government, whose population sets the record for HIV infections, came under pressure for its refusal to admit there is any connection with AIDS because of the cost it would have involved. In the United States 12% to 16% of the citizens do not have health insurance. State boards and the Department of Health regulate inpatient care to reduce the national health care deficit. To tackle the problems of the perpetually increasing number of uninsured, and costs associated with the US health care system, President Barack Obama says he favors the creation of a universal health care system.

However, *New York Times* opinion columnist Paul Krugman said that Obama's plan would not actually provide universal coverage, and Factcheck.org alleges that Obama's predicted savings were exaggerated. In contrast, the state of Oregon and the city of San Francisco are both examples of governments that adopted universal healthcare systems for strictly fiscal reasons.

Target Populations

Health care systems are composed of individuals and organizations that aim to meet the health care needs of target populations. There are a wide variety of health care systems around the world. In some countries, the health care system planning is distributed among market participants, whereas in others planning is made more centrally among governments, trade unions, charities, religious, or other co-ordinated bodies to deliver planned health care services targeted to the populations they serve. However, health care planning has often been evolutionary rather than revolutionary.

SPECIAL SERVICES FOR HEALTH TOURISTS

Services typically sought by travelers include elective procedures as well as complex specialized surgeries such as joint replacement (knee/hip), cardiac surgery, dental surgery, and cosmetic surgeries. However, virtually every type of health care, including psychiatry, alternative treatments, convalescent care and even burial services are available.

Over 50 countries have identified medical tourism as a national industry. However, accreditation and other measures of quality vary widely across the globe, and some destinations may become hazardous or even dangerous for medical tourists.

In the context of global health, "medical tourism" is a

pejorative because during such trips health care providers often practice outside of their areas of expertise or hold different (i.e., lower) standards of care. Greater numbers than ever before of student volunteers, health professions trainees, and researchers from resource-rich countries are working temporarily and anticipating future work in resource-starved areas. This emphasizes the importance of understanding this other definition.

The concept of medical tourism is not a new one. The first recorded instance of medical tourism dates back thousands of years to when Greek pilgrims traveled from all over the Mediterranean to the small territory in the Saronic Gulf called Epidauria. This territory was the sanctuary of the healing god Asklepios. Epidauria became the original travel destination for medical tourism.

Spa towns and sanitariums may be considered an early form of medical tourism. In eighteenth century England, for example, patients visited spas because they were places with supposedly health-giving mineral waters, treating diseases from gout to liver disorders and bronchitis.

Medical Travel

Factors that have led to the increasing popularity of medical travel include the high cost of health care, long wait times for certain procedures, the ease and affordability of international travel, and improvements in both technology and standards of care in many countries. Cost seems to play an important role in the occurrence of medical tourism, many surgery procedures performed overseas cost a fraction of the price they do in America. For example a liver transplant that cost $300,000 USD in America cost about $91,000 USD in Taiwan.

A large draw to medical travel is convenience and speed. Countries that operate public health-care systems are often so taxed that it can take considerable time to get non-urgent medical care. Using Canada as an example, an estimated

782,936 Canadians spent time on medical waiting lists in 2005, waiting an average of 9.4 weeks. Canada has set waiting-time benchmarks, e. g. 26 weeks for a hip replacement and 16 weeks for cataract surgery, for non-urgent medical procedures.

Medical tourists can come from anywhere in the First World, including Europe, the Middle East, Japan, the United States, and Canada. This is because of their large populations, comparatively high wealth, the high expense of health care or lack of health care options locally, and increasingly high expectations of their populations with respect to health care.

An authority at the Harvard Business School recently stated that "medical tourism is promoted much more heavily in the United Kingdom than in the United States". A forecast by Deloitte Consulting published in August 2008 projected that medical tourism originating in the US could jump by a factor of ten over the next decade. An estimated 750,000 Americans went abroad for health care in 2007, and the report estimated that a million and a half would seek health care outside the US in 2008. The growth in medical tourism has the potential to cost US health care providers billions of dollars in lost revenue.

Additionally, patients are finding that insurance either does not cover orthopedic surgery (such as knee/hip replacement) or imposes unreasonable restrictions on the choice of the facility, surgeon, or prosthetics to be used. Medical tourism for knee/hip replacements has emerged as one of the more widely accepted procedures because of the lower cost and minimal difficulties associated with the traveling to/from the surgery.

Colombia provides a knee replacement for about $5,000 USD, including all associated fees, such as FDA-approved prosthetics and hospital stay-over expenses. However, many clinics quote prices that are not all-inclusive and include only the surgeon fees associated with the procedure.

According to an article by the University of Delaware publication, UDaily:

" The cost of surgery in India, Thailand or South Africa can be one-tenth of what it is in the United States or Western Europe, and sometimes even less. A heart-valve replacement that would cost $200,000 or more in the US, for example, goes for $10,000 in India—and that includes round-trip airfare and a brief vacation package. Similarly, a metal-free dental bridge worth $5,500 in the US costs $500 in India, a knee replacement in Thailand with six days of physical therapy costs about one-fifth of what it would in the States, and Lasik eye surgery worth $3,700 in the US is available in many other countries for only $730. Cosmetic surgery savings are even greater: A full facelift that would cost $20,000 in the US runs about $1,250 in South Africa."

Popular medical travel worldwide destinations include: Argentina, Brunei, Cuba, Colombia, Costa Rica, Hong Kong, Hungary, India, Jordan, Lithuania, Malaysia, The Philippines, Singapore, South Africa, Thailand, and recently, Saudi Arabia, UAE, South Korea, Tunisia and New Zealand.

Popular cosmetic surgery travel destinations include: Argentina, Bolivia, Brazil, Colombia, Costa Rica, Cuba, Mexico and Turkey. In South America, countries such as Argentina, Bolivia, Brazil and Colombia lead on plastic surgery medical skills relying on their experienced plastic surgeons. In Bolivia and Colombia, plastic surgery has also become quite common. According to the "Sociedad Boliviana de Cirugia Plastica y Reconstructiva", more than 70% of middle and upper class women in the country have had some form of plastic surgery. Colombia also provides advanced care in cardiovascular and transplant surgery.

In Europe Belgium, Poland and Slovakia are also breaking into the business. South Africa is taking the term "medical tourism" very literally by promoting their "medical safaris".

A specialized subset of medical tourism is reproductive tourism and reproductive outsourcing, which is the practice of traveling abroad to undergo in-vitro fertilization, surrogate pregnancy and other assisted reproductive technology treatments including freezing embryos for retro-production.

However, perceptions of medical tourism are not always positive. In places like the US, which has high standards of quality, medical tourism is viewed as risky. In some parts of the world, wider political issues can influence where medical tourists will choose to seek out health care.

Health tourism providers have developed as intermediaries to unite potential medical tourists with provider hospitals and other organisations. Companies are beginning to offer global health care options that will enable North American and European patients to access world health care at a fraction of the cost of domestic care. Companies that focus on medical value travel typically provide nurse case managers to assist patients with pre- and post-travel medical issues. They also help provide resources for follow-up care upon the patient's return.

Typical Process

The typical process is as follows: the person seeking medical treatment abroad contacts a medical tourism provider. The provider usually requires the patient to provide a medical report, including the nature of ailment, local doctor's opinion, medical history, and diagnosis, and may request additional information. Certified medical doctors or consultants then advise on the medical treatment. The approximate expenditure, choice of hospitals and tourist destinations, and duration of stay, etc., is discussed.

After signing consent bonds and agreements, the patient is given recommendation letters for a medical visa, to be procured from the concerned embassy. The patient travels to the destination country, where the medical tourism provider assigns a case executive, who takes care of the patient's accommodation, treatment and any other form of care. Once the treatment is done, the patient can remain in the tourist destination or return home.

International Healthcare Accreditation

The oldest international accrediting body is Accreditation Canada, formerly known as the Canadian Council on Health Services Accreditation, which accredited the Bermuda Hospital Board as soon as 1968. Since then, it has accredited hospitals and health service organizations in ten other countries.

In the United States, the best known accreditation group is the Joint Commission International (JCI). They have been inspecting and accrediting health care facilities and hospitals outside of the United States since 1999. Many international hospitals today see obtaining international accreditation as a way to attract American patients.

Joint Commission International is a relative of the Joint Commission in the United States. Both are independent private sector not-for-profit organizations that develop nationally and internationally recognized procedures and standards to help improve patient care and safety. They work with hospitals to help them meet Joint Commission standards for patient care and then accredit those hospitals meeting the standards.

QHA Trent Accreditation, based in the UK, is an active accreditation scheme. Prior to that, the Trent International Accreditation Scheme was a key player.

The different international healthcare accreditation schemes vary in quality, size, cost, intent and the skill and intensity of their marketing. They also vary in terms of cost to hospitals and healthcare institutions making use of them. A forecast by Deloitte Consulting regarding medical tourism published in August 2008 noted the value of accreditation in ensuring quality of healthcare and specifically mentioned JCI, ISQUA and Trent.

Increasingly, some hospitals are looking towards dual international accreditation, perhaps having both JCI to cover potential US clientele, Trent for potential British and European clientele and Accreditation Canada. As a result of competition between clinics for American medical tourists, there have been initiatives to rank hospitals based on patient-reported metrics.

Other organizations providing contributions to quality practices include:

- The United Kingdom Accreditation Forum (UKAF) is an established network of accreditation organisations with the intention of sharing experience good practice and new ideas around the methodology for accreditation programmes, covering issues such as developing healthcare quality standards, implementation of standards within healthcare organisations, assessment by peer review and exploration of the peer review techniques to include the recruitment, training, monitoring and evaluation of peer reviewers and the mechanisms for awards of accredited status to organisations.

ORGANIZATIONS AND ASSOCIATIONS

Medical Tourism Association (MTA), the first for-profit trade association for medical tourism, is made up of international hospitals, healthcare providers, medical travel facilitators, insurance companies, and other affiliated companies and members with the common goal of promoting medical tourism in a global environment. The Association promotes the interests of its healthcare provider and medical travel facilitator members. The MTA has three tenets: Transparency, Communication and Education. The goal of these types of associations is often to raise awareness of medical tourism in the hopes of expanding the industry.

HealthCare Tourism International (HTI) is a 501(c) non-profit organization that is complementary to the Joint Commission International accreditation group. Health care organizations can apply for self-certification or accreditation on the HTI website.

Risks

Medical tourism carries some risks that locally-provided medical care does not. Some countries, such as India, Malaysia, or Thailand have very different infectious disease-related epidemiology to Europe and North America. Exposure to diseases without having built up natural immunity can be a hazard for weakened individuals, specifically with respect to gastrointestinal diseases (e.g. Hepatitis A, amoebic dysentery, paratyphoid) which could weaken progress, mosquito-transmitted diseases, influenza, and tuberculosis. However, because in poor tropical nations diseases run the gamut, doctors seem to be more open to the possibility of considering any infectious disease, including HIV, TB, and typhoid, while there are cases in the West where patients were consistently misdiagnosed for years because such diseases are perceived to be "rare" in the West.

The quality of post-operative care can also vary dramatically, depending on the hospital and country, and may be different from US or European standards. However, JCI and Trent fulfill the role of accreditation by assessing the standards in the healthcare in the countries like India, China and Thailand. Also, traveling long distances soon after surgery can increase the risk of complications. Long flights and decreased mobility in a cramped airline cabin are a known risk factor for developing blood clots in the legs such as venous thrombosis or pulmonary embolus economy class syndrome. Other vacation activities can be problematic as well — for example, scars may become darker and more noticeable if they sunburn while healing. To minimise these problems, medical tourism patients often combine their medical trips with vacation time set aside for rest and recovery in the destination country.

Also, health facilities treating medical tourists may lack an adequate complaints policy to deal appropriately and fairly with complaints made by dissatisfied patients.

Differences in healthcare provider standards around the world have been recognised by the World Health Organization, and in 2004 it launched the World Alliance for Patient Safety. This body assists hospitals and government around the world in setting patient safety policy and practices that can become particularly relevant when providing medical tourism services.

Finally, after returning home, a patient will have limited contact with his or her surgeon. This means that it will be difficult to deal with any complications that may arise later such as a delayed infection.

Legal Issues

Receiving medical care abroad may subject medical tourists to unfamiliar legal issues. The limited nature of litigation in various countries is one reason for the lower cost of care overseas. While some countries currently presenting themselves as attractive medical tourism destinations provide some form of legal remedies for medical malpractice, these legal avenues may be unappealing to the medical tourist. Should problems arise, patients might not be covered by adequate personal insurance or might be unable to seek compensation via malpractice lawsuits. Hospitals and/or doctors in some countries may be unable to pay the financial damages awarded by a court to a patient who has sued them, owing to the hospital and/or the doctor not possessing appropriate insurance cover and/or medical indemnity.

Ethical Issues

There can be major ethical issues around medical tourism. For example, the illegal purchase of organs and tissues for transplantation had been alleged in countries such as India and China prior to 2007. The Declaration of Istanbul distinguishes between ethically problematic "transplant tourism" and "travel for transplantation".

Medical tourism may raise broader ethical issues for the countries in which it is promoted. For example in India, some argue that a "policy of 'medical tourism for the classes and health missions for the masses' will lead to a deepening of the inequities" already embedded in the health care system. In Thailand, in 2008 it was stated that, "Doctors in Thailand have become so busy with foreigners that Thai patients are having trouble getting care". Medical tourism centred on new technologies, such as stem cell treatments, is often criticized on grounds of fraud, blatant lack of scientific rationale and patient safety. However, when pioneering advanced technologies, such as providing 'unproven' therapies to patients outside of regular clinical trials, it is often challenging to differentiate between acceptable medical innovation and unacceptable patient exploitation.

2

HEALTH TOURISTS

Thailand is one of the most popular tourist destinations from Southeast Asia attracting around 15 million tourists every year. Healthl tourism has added yet another dimension to its tourism popularity due to growing demand for low-priced cosmetic and other treatments in western countries. Services typically sought by tourists in Thailand include cheap plastic surgeries to more serious life-saving medical procedures. Statics indicate that the cost of surgery in Thailand can be one-tenth of what it is in Australia or United States.

Popular medical treatments and plastic surgeries in Thailand include breast implants and breast augmentations surgeries. Thousands of patients travel to Thailand, particularly from Latin America, Europe and Australia. They are lured by the repute of Thailand doctors, extremely low prices added to high levels of personalized care, world renowned rich and mystical cultural heritage.

Tough new restrictions to stop so-called health tourists taking the NHS "for a ride" have been unveiled by the Government.

The rule changes, which follow a three-month public consultation, will mean many visitors to the UK, including failed asylum seekers and business travellers, will have to pay for treatment except in genuine emergencies.

The Department of Health said health tourism was a significant problem in many parts of the country. It is believed it costs the NHS around £200 million a year.

Medical leaders and opposition MPs criticised the plans, saying there was little evidence on the extent of the problem and doctors did not want to act as "state agents" in policing patients.

The Department of Health said the action aimed to close existing loopholes which have allowed overseas visitors with no substantive link to the UK to have often expensive treatments free in NHS hospitals.

These include foreigners who come to the UK on a business trip only to "suddenly discover" they are ill and need treatment. The rules will also stop heavily pregnant women who have relatives permanently resident in the UK coming here just to give birth.

The changes, which come into force in April, will also stop failed asylum seekers and others with no legal right to be in the country from receiving free treatment for illnesses which arise after their legal status has been finally determined.

Health minister John Hutton said the changes were supported by NHS staff who wanted to protect resources for those entitled to them.

He said NHS staff would now have a "clear set of rules" to comply with and NHS trusts were expected to enforce them properly to "ensure that NHS resources are used to meet the healthcare needs of people living in the UK, not those who just happen to be passing through".

Mr Hutton said the NHS Counter Fraud Service would help pursue those who falsely claimed entitlement to free treatment on the NHS.

SAFETY CONCERN

Health tourists rate safety as their number one concern when choosing their holiday destination according to new data released today by the FIA on World Tourism Day.

Lack of safety whether due to crime, the risk of natural disasters, sanitary risks or terrorism, was the principle reason to rule out a destination, and scored highest in the survey with 8.5 points out of a possible 10. Safety was closely followed by weather which received an average 8.2 points, quality of accommodation received 8.2 points, and natural beauty 8.0 points.

The data, based on a survey conducted by the FIA, highlighted the need for tourism organisations and governments to ensure that tourists are provided with adequate information on the areas with a higher risk, maximise security measures, and establish common information and evacuation protocols for all countries in cases of disaster or health risks.

The factors that were the least valued by tourists in choosing a destination included the availability of sports facilities (4.8) and nightlife (4.9), although the latter was the highest valued factor among travellers aged 18 to 30 years. Likewise, availability of sports facilities was more important for tourists aged 18 to 45 than those aged 46 and older.

Presence of natural beauty in the surrounding area, including quality of beaches and other swimming areas, scored significantly higher in importance than quality of food or other tourist attractions.

The survey also revealed that most tourists travelled to countries within their own continent. For example Southern Europe was noted as the most frequent destination region of European travellers. However, younger respondents from 18 to 30 years old travelled to a greater degree to destinations outside of Europe compared with older respondents.

"Although in principle the care of foreign and local patients should essentially be the same and fit the best possible standards, there is evidence that it is not always so," ESHRE's Francoise Shenfield told reporters at a briefing.

A survey of 105 countries by the IFFS found that cultural, religious and social differences in attitudes to fertility treatments such as using donated eggs, sperm or embryos mean there are wide variations in the number of clinics that offer treatment, and the services they provide.

In vitro fertilization (IVF) involves removing eggs from a woman's ovaries and combining them with sperm in a lab. The strongest embryos are then implanted into a woman's womb. In theory, the eggs, sperm and embryos can all be donated.

The IFFS survey found there are over 500 fertility clinics in India and about 615 in Japan, but only 66 in Britain, 120 in Germany, 200 in Spain and around 360 in Italy.

IFFS education director Ian Cooke said discrepancies in access prompted patients to travel abroad for treatment, but could leave them in medical, financial or legal difficulties.

LEGAL DIFFERENCES

One major problem is the rules on the maximum number of embryos that can be transferred to a woman's womb after IVF.

In Britain and Scandinavia only one or two are allowed, but other countries have higher limits or none at all -- a factor that can increase the number of multiple pregnancies that can pose risks for both mothers and babies.

Freezing embryos is banned in Germany, Italy and Croatia, but freezing eggs before they are fertilized is allowed. In Britain the removal of donors' anonymity has led to a severe shortage in donated sperm.

Sperm and egg donation is banned completely in many Islamic countries, and in France lesbians are not allowed access to donated sperm. Turkey has recently banned anyone going abroad to receive donated sperm or eggs -- a law which the experts said was almost completely unenforceable.

"If a woman goes on holiday and comes back pregnant, who is to tell exactly how or when she got pregnant?" said Shenfield.

Both IFFS and ESHRE support the rights of patients to travel to receive fertility treatment, but said in a joint statement that "ideally, this should take place in their home country."

They urged national health authorities to try to harmonize standards to increase the safety of patients and offer equal treatment for all those who want it.

"The variation in international laws relating to infertility treatment is one of the reasons that cause couples to seek cross-border treatment," said Cooke. "Whilst this is unavoidable we call for international standards to ensure these patients receive consistent advice and safe treatment."

Destination of Thailand

Seekers of medical ailments get to explore exotic and culturally distinct destinations spread throughout its 76 provinces ranging from mountainous north to sultry south. Tourism authority of Thailand aims at promoting Thailand medical tourism as a global centre of excellence in medical tourism industry. The body has listed several accredited hospitals, clinics, spas and Thai traditional medicine practitioners for tourists to easily locate and avail credible and safe medical services in Thailand.

There are around 700 government and 300 private hospitals and thanks to their efficient, cost-effective and luxurious health care facilities, tourists can combine health and holiday aspects of travel and enjoy great savings in time and money.

Thailand has glorious beaches, tropical climate, delicious cuisine and friendly people, all adding to an unforgettable experience. Tourists can easily plan and organize their entire trip with health and holiday partners for all transfers, hotel accommodations, appointment with doctors, healthcare treatment bookings, sightseeing tours as well as entertainment attractions.

From exotic beaches and islands, to eco-tourism, historical sightseeing, astounding nightlife and several excursion trips, Thailand can provide a precise combination of excellent, exotic locales and leisure that you may desire.

A significant proportion of medical tourism and medical travel is driven by people seeking established and proven treatments in countries where the cost of the treatment or operation is much lower than in their home country. Within this segment of the market, the focus of patient safety is upon the hospital, clinic or doctor who is carrying out the treatment. Can the patient be confident that the healthcare provider has the necessary expertise and experience to carry out the procedure? The question... "Does this treatment actually work?" does not arise.

Swiss hospitals and clinics are increasingly looking over the border for patients, especially to countries in which the wealthy want high standards of medical care.

Health tourists from Russia and the Middle East are among those attracted to Switzerland to both private clinics and university hospitals. China is a future target.

The number of these patients is on the rise, say those in the hospital sector, even if no exact national figures exist at present.

"There are an estimated 30,000 foreign patients who come to Switzerland every year for medical care, not counting people from the border areas," said Gregor Frei, who heads Swiss Health. The platform was set up in 2008 by the Swiss trade promotion umbrella organisation, Osec, to promote Swiss healthcare providers abroad.

There are no detailed economic figures either, but Frei says it is possible to make an approximate calculation.

"Medical treatment can cost SFr20,000 ($22,000) a day. This sum can be multiplied five to ten times, taking into account overnight stays in luxury hotels for those accompanying the patient, shopping and other generous expenses."

"The countries which we are concentrating on at the moment are the Gulf States and Russia: soon we will also include the Far East, especially China."

Increase Visibility

Swiss Health encourages its members to increase their visibility through participation in medical conferences - for example in Saudi Arabia, Russian and Oman - and by collaborating with Swiss embassies, chambers of commerce, foreign health ministers and specialists in the health sector.

The Ars Medica Hospital Group, which has two clinics in the Lugano area in the southern canton of Ticino, is among those with patients from abroad.

"Foreign patients account for more than five per cent of all our customers, a percentage that keeps rising compared with previous years," said Jérôme Puginier, director of services at the group.

"Our foreign patients mainly come from northern Italy, but for several years the number coming from Russia has been increasing."

Word of Mouth

Ars Medica has a strategy to boost its visibility. "In addition to taking part in conferences and collaboration with foreign doctors who refer their patients, the best advertising is definitely the excellent service," Puginier said.

"Happy patients will carry out word-of-mouth advertising among their friends and family, which is efficient publicity."

Rich health tourists come to Switzerland for many sorts of health care, says Swiss Health's Frei.

"This clientele is looking for top standards across all the medical sectors, and not in any particular discipline," he said.

Puginier agrees. "It's difficult to draw up a league table because the pathologies we treat are very diverse: from orthopaedic surgery to gynaecology, as well as obstetrics, neonatal medicine, surgery, internal medicine and oncology. Not forgetting reproductive medicine and cosmetic surgery."

High Quality

There are two types of health tourism, he adds. "There's one based on getting good value for money and there's the other based on getting the best quality."

"As Switzerland is already known for having one of the best health services in the world - excellent care, cutting edge infrastructure, almost total lack of waiting lists - we must nevertheless strengthen this position as a high-level health destination."

Ars Medica has created a Centre for Preventive Medicine for foreign clients. "The day-long health status assessment includes biological and genetic analysis, diagnostic imaging, functional testing, physiotherapy and dietary consultancy and a final report with personalised recommendations," explained Puginier.

The basic package - also presented in Russian on the group's website - costs around SFr3,000.

Public Hospitals Too

Given spiralling health costs, public hospitals are also turning their attention to this lucrative source of income - those in Zurich, Bern, Basel and Geneva are all members of Swiss Health.

Conrad Engler, from the Swiss Hospital Association, plays down the question of whether these clinics have sufficient infrastructure.

"The decisive argument in attracting patients is Switzerland's leading-edge services, especially in the university hospitals," he said.

"Health marketing and other 'collateral' aspects are not key influences. What counts is the reputation for quality: for example, the international reputation of the oncologist Franco Cavalli brings patients from all over the world to Ticino."

For proven treatments, the hospitals, clinics and doctors (and medical tourism facilitators) can reassure the patient by providing proof of qualifications, accreditations; experience and so on.... and in some cases may be prepared to provide data on clinical outcomes. Unfortunately, this is all too often lacking. Patients are often asked to take on trust the claims of the healthcare provider, particularly in those countries that do not have national standards and systems for the collection of comparative clinical outcome data or independent review and analysis. Even an international accreditation such as JCI is not a guarantee of quality, nor an assessment of how good a hospital actually is at delivering safe and successful treatments.

So, in established areas of medical travel such as cosmetic surgery, dental treatment and elective surgery there is still much work to be done to convince potential medical tourists that treatment abroad is a safe option (or at least as safe as within their home country).

Dental Tourist

Dental tourism is a subset of the sector known as medical tourism. Also found under the heading of Dental Vacations. It involves individuals seeking dental care outside of their local healthcare systems usually in combination with taking a vacation to a foreign country.

While dental tourists may travel for a variety of reasons, their choices are usually driven by price considerations. Wide variations in the economics of countries with shared borders have been the historical mainstay of the sector. Examples include travel from Austria to Hungary, Slovakia and Slovenia, the US to Mexico, from the Republic of Ireland to Northern Ireland,Hungary,Turkey and Poland.

While medical tourism is often generalized to travel from high-income countries to low-cost developing economies, other factors can influence a decision to travel, including differences between the funding of public healthcare or general access to healthcare.

TONGUE CLEANING

Cleaning the tongue as part of daily oral hygiene is essential, since it removes the white/yellow bad-breath-generating coating of bacteria, decaying food particles, fungi (such as Candida), and dead cells from the dorsal area of the tongue. Tongue cleaning also removes some of the bacteria species which generate tooth decay and gum problems.

Gum Care

Massaging gums with toothbrush bristles is generally recommended for good oral health. Flossing is recommended at least once per day, preferably before bed, to help prevent receding gums, gum disease, and cavities between the teeth.

Oral Irrigation

Some dental professionals recommend oral irrigation as a way to clean teeth and gums.

Oral irrigators reach 3-4 mm under the gum line. Oral irrigators use a pressured, directed stream of water to disrupt plaque and bacteria.

FOOD AND DRINK

Foods that help muscles and bones also help teeth and gums. Breads and cereals are rich in vitamin B while fruits and vegetables contain vitamin C, both of which contribute to healthy gum tissue.(8) Lean meat, fish, and poultry provide magnesium and zinc for teeth. Some people recommend that teeth be brushed after every meal and at bedtime, and flossed at least once per day, preferably at night before sleep. For some people, flossing might be recommended after every meal.

Beneficial Foods

Some foods may protect against cavities. Fluoride is a primary protector against dental cavities. Fluoride makes the surface of teeth more resistant to acids during the process of remineralisation. Drinking fluoridated water is recommended by some dental professionals while others say that using toothpaste alone is enough. Milk and cheese are also rich in calcium and phosphate, and may also encourage remineralisation.

All foods increase saliva production, and since saliva contains buffer chemicals this helps to stabilize the pH to near 7 (neutral) in the mouth. Foods high in fiber may also help to increase the flow of saliva. Sugar-free chewing gum stimulates saliva production, and helps to clean the surface of the teeth.(8)

According to World Dental, these are the top ten beneficial foods for teeth.

1. Green tea contains polyphenol antioxidant plant compounds that reduce plaque and help reduce cavities and gum disease. Tea may help reduce bad breath. Tooth enamel is strengthened because green tea contains fluoride which promotes healthy teeth.
2. Milk and yogurt are good for teeth because they contain low acidity, which means that wearing of teeth is less.

They are also low in decay-inducing sugar. Milk is a good source of calcium, the main component of teeth and bones.

3. Cheese contains calcium and phosphate, which helps balance pH in the mouth preserves (and rebuilds) tooth enamel, produces saliva, and kills bacteria that cause cavities and disease.
4. Fruits such as apples, strawberries and kiwis contain Vitamin C. This vitamin is considered the element that holds cells together. If this vitamin is neglected, gum cells can break down, making gums tender and susceptible to disease.
5. Vegetables: Vitamin A, found in pumpkins, carrots, sweet potatoes and broccoli, is necessary for the formation of tooth enamel. Crunchy vegetables may also help clean gums.
6. Onions contain antibacterial sulfur compounds. Tests show that onions kill various types of bacteria, especially when eaten raw.
7. Celery protects teeth by producing saliva which neutralizes bacteria that cause cavities. It also massages the teeth and gums.
8. Sesame seeds reduce plaque and help build tooth enamel. They are also very high in calcium.
9. Animal food: beef, chicken, turkey, and eggs contain phosphorus which, with calcium, is one of the two most vital minerals of teeth and bone.
10. Water cleans the mouth and produces saliva that deposits essential minerals into the teeth. It keeps teeth hydrated and washes away particles from the teeth.

Dental Cavities

Sugars are commonly associated with dental cavities. Other carbohydrates, especially cooked starches, e.g. crisps/

potato chips, may also damage teeth, although to a lesser degree since starch has to be converted by enzymes in saliva first.

Sucrose (table sugar) is most commonly associated with cavities. The amount of sugar consumed at any one time is less important than how often food and drinks that contain sugar are consumed. The more frequently sugars are consumed, the greater the time during which the tooth is exposed to low pH levels, at which point demineralisation occurs (below 5.5 for most people).

It is important therefore to try to encourage infrequent consumption of food and drinks containing sugar so that teeth have a chance to be repaired by remineralisation and fluoride. Limiting sugar-containing foods and drinks to meal times is one way to reduce the incidence of cavities. Sugars from fruit and fruit juices, e.g., glucose, fructose, and maltose seem equally likely to cause cavities.

Acids contained in fruit juice, vinegar and soft drinks lower the pH level of the oral cavity which causes the enamel to demineralize. Drinking drinks such as orange juice or cola throughout the day raises the risk of dental cavities tremendously.

Another factor which affects the risk of developing cavities is the stickiness of foods. Some foods or sweets may stick to the teeth and so reduce the pH in the mouth for an extended time, particularly if they are sugary. It is important that teeth be cleaned at least twice a day, preferably with a toothbrush and fluoride toothpaste, to remove any food sticking to the teeth. Regular brushing and the use of dental floss also removes the dental plaque coating the tooth surface.

Chewing gum assists oral irrigation between and around the teeth, cleaning and removing particles, but for teeth in poor condition it may damage or remove loose fillings as well.

Effect of Smoking

Smoking and chewing tobacco are both strongly linked with multiple dental diseases. Regular vomiting, as seen in bulimia nervosa, also causes significant damage.

Mouthwash or mouth rinse improve oral hygiene. Dental chewing gums claim to improve dental health.

WAYS TO ATTRACT MORE TOURISTS

Indian travel companies are getting practical. Realising that Phuket, Colombo, Kathmandu and Genting Heights are attracting far more tourists from Western countries, and also that the Indian tourism season has shrunk to six months (October-March), some travel companies are devising innovative ways to attract more tourists.

So, while shack owners in Goa give their shacks a makeover after Diwali , tour agents in Assam do up their boats to offer the Brahmaputra cruise to European travellers.

Yet others, like the non-profit Mata Vaishno Devi Shrine Board is trying to provide the best pilgrimage experience to Non-Resident Indians from all over the world.

This explains why all such players were seen sharing corners of the same convention centre at Pragati Maidan last week at the South Asia Travel and Tourism Exchange (SATTE) conference.

"Twenty-five buyers have made inquiries about bird-watching in Assam and Meghalaya since yesterday. We organise these trips for a group of four or more for $80 per day inclusive of everything but the airfare to Guwahati," says Arijit Purkayastha, general manager-tours, Network Travels.

These trips are highly popular among Europeans and there are packages for six nights-seven days or nine nights-10 days. Network also arranges individual travels for $110 per day.

For the people of Thailand and China, there is a déjà vu trip to the interiors of the northeastern states, where their ancestors once lived.

"Not many know that there is a mini-Thailand and a mini-China in India, both of which are of great nostalgic value to the people of these countries, and we offer a lot of personal touches to tourists coming to these places," says Nimalya Chowdhury, senior executive-tours, Jungle Travels India.

The company also organises luxury river cruises on the Brahmaputra, and a four night-five day tour ideally costs Rs 16,000.

Chowdhury is elated because he has bagged 10 bookings for the end of May at the SATTE conference. He also boasts that last year, 400 tourists took the Assam Bengal cruise for which his company charges $215 per day per person.

Driven by the good response, the tour company is planning to raise prices to $245 per person. And this also means good business for a whole lot of tour operators.

The larger the group, the larger the commission for a tour operator who gets these tourists. For instance, for a smaller group, the tour operator's commission is 10-15 per cent but it may go up to 25 per cent when the group comprises more than 20 persons.

Yet there are others, like Sterling Resorts, which have moved beyond their traditional resort selling through time shares. They are promoting their hotels as eco-friendly and have also come up with two heritage hotels in Thanjavur and Mahabalipuram.

"We have converted two entire villages near these cities into heritage villages where tourists live like villagers, wearing the same kinds of clothes, eating the same kinds of food in similar vessels and going through similar massages, yoga, medidation baths and chores," says Colonel PS James, president, Indeco.

According to Col James, besides foreigners, the concept is becoming very popular among rich and well-settled Indians whose roots are in such villages and who want to revisit their childhood.

He also asserts that this is different from Chokhi Dhani near Jaipur , where an artificial village has been created. The rates for these stays typically start at $90 per day per person including meals.

Similar concepts are being floated in the newly formed state of Chhattisgarh where model villages are being created for tourism purposes.

There is also a proposal to convert an old jail into a hotel which will retain the essential fabric of a jail so that tourists get the experience of being a jail inmate, wearing pyjamas like a prisoners and eating food in distorted vessels.

"The number of tourists visiting the Bastar region has risen from 2,000 to 10,000 in two years, says an official representing the state at the SATTE conference.

And multinational hotels seem be taking lessons in indigenisation from these smaller players. Delhi's [Images] Japanese hotel, Nikko, for instance, has added an Indian restaurant called Chutney in its bid to attract customers having a taste for Indian food. Its earlier restaurant, Sakura, only served Japanese food.

However, it is not about making profit all the time. For instance, Shri Mata Vaishno Devi Shrine Board is making every effort to offer the pilgrims visiting Vaishno Devi temple the best darshan.

Now targeting NRIs, the board is providing every possible facility for pilgrims to have a satisfying visit to the shrine. "We have a tie-up with SBI. ATM card holders for prior bookings and have started golf cart services for older people," says Rajesh Raina, an official at the board.

And what is ISKON doing at SATTE? "It is an opportunity for us sell our books," says a worker. Not many are aware that if you are a life member you can stay in any of its temples for three nights-four days free of cost, all over the world.

Similarly, countries with a low profile in India, like Sri Lanka , Egypt and Poland, are doing their bit to attract outbound tourists. The Egyptian Tourism Authority (ETA) has opened an office in Mumbai .

"We are getting around 50,000 tourists from India, which we expect to double in 2005-06," says Samy Mehmoud of ETA.

And even Poland is coming up with new attractions. "While 30 million tourists visit Poland every year, Indians comprise less than 10,000. We are popularising Poland amongst Indian through promotional schemes," says Wlodzimierz Madziar, second secretary, Embassy of Poland.

3

SLASHING THE HIGH COST OF HEALTH CARE

Rising health care costs and-consequently-the large number of uninsured have become two of the most prominent public policy issues in the presidential campaign. Before politicians attempt to "solve" the problem, they should first understand what is driving it.

The relentless, decades-long rise in the cost of health care has left many Americans struggling to pay their medical bills. Workers complain that they cannot afford high premiums for health insurance. Patients forgo recommended care rather than pay the out-of-pocket costs.

Employers are cutting back or eliminating health benefits, forcing millions more people into the ranks of the uninsured. And state and federal governments strain to meet the expanding costs of public programs like Medicaid and Medicare.

Health care costs are far higher in the United States than in any other advanced nation, whether measured in total dollars spent, as a percentage of the economy, or on a per capita basis. And health costs here have been rising significantly faster than the overall economy or personal incomes for more than 40 years, a trend that cannot continue forever.

It is the worst long-term fiscal crisis facing the nation, and it demands a solution, but finding one will not be easy or palatable.

THE CAUSES

Varied and Deep-Rooted

Contrary to popular beliefs, this is not a problem driven mainly by the aging of the baby boom generation, or the high cost of prescription drugs, or medical malpractice litigation that spawns defensive medicine. Those issues often dominate political discourse, but they have played relatively minor roles in driving up medical spending in this country and abroad. The major causes are much more deep-seated and far harder to root out.

Almost all economists would agree that the main driver of high medical spending here is our wealth. We are richer than other countries and so willing to spend more. But authoritative analyses have found that we spend well above what mere wealth would predict.

This is mostly because we pay hospitals and doctors more than most other countries do. We rely more on costly specialists, who overuse advanced technologies, like CT scans and M.R.I. machines, and who resort to costly surgical or medical procedures a lot more than doctors in other countries do.

Perverse insurance incentives entice doctors and patients to use expensive medical services more than is warranted. And our fragmented array of insurers and providers eats up a lot of money in administrative costs, marketing expenses and profits that do not afflict government-run systems abroad.

Does It Matter?

If citizens of an extremely wealthy nation like the United States want to spend more on health care and less on a third car, a new computer or a vacation home, what's wrong with that? By some measures, Americans are getting good value.

Studies by reputable economists have concluded that spending on such advanced treatments as cardiac drugs, devices and surgery; neonatal care for low-birth-weight infants; and mental health drugs have more than paid for themselves by extending lives and improving their quality.

But if health care spending continues on its same trajectory, the United States will reach the point - probably several decades from now - where every penny of the annual increase in gross domestic product would have to go for health care. There would be less and less money for other things, like education, environmental protection, scientific research and national security, that may be equally or more important to the well-being of society.

Governmental budgets will face the crisis even sooner. States are already complaining that they have to crimp other vital activities, like education, to meet soaring Medicaid costs.

And federal spending on Medicare and Medicaid is surging upward at rates that will cause the deficit to soar. That means politicians will have to raise taxes, severely cut a wide range of other governmental programs, or chop back the health programs themselves.

The question is: What can be done to lower both the high level of health care spending and its high rate of increase from year to year?

The Solutions

Geography

Pioneering studies by researchers at Dartmouth have shown enormous disparities in expenditures on health care from one region to another with no discernible difference in health outcomes. Doctors in high-cost areas use hospitals, costly technology and platoons of consulting physicians a lot more often than doctors in low-cost areas, yet their patients, on average, fare no better. There are hints that they may even do worse because they pick up infections in the hospital and because having a horde of doctors can mean no one is in charge.

If the entire nation could bring its costs down to match the lower-spending regions, the country could cut perhaps 20 to 30 percent off its health care bill, a tremendous saving. That would require changing the long- ingrained practices of the medical profession. Public and private insurers might need to refuse coverage for high-cost care that adds little value.

Stick to What Works

The sad truth is that less than half of all medical care in the United States is supported by good evidence that it works, according to estimates cited by the Congressional Budget Office. If doctors had better information on which treatments work best for which patients, and whether the benefits were commensurate with the costs, needless treatment could be junked, the savings could be substantial, and patient care would surely improve. It could take a decade, or several, to conduct comparative-effectiveness studies, modify relevant laws, and change doctors' behavior.

Managed Care

For a brief period in the 1990s it looked as if health maintenance organizations competing for patients and carefully managing their care might bring down costs and improve quality at the same time. The H.M.O.'s did help restrain costs for a few years. The problem was, doctors and patients hated the system, management became much looser, and the upsurge in costs resumed. Managed care techniques are creeping back into some health plans, especially for services apt to be overused, but too heavy a hand would most likely produce another backlash.

Information Technologies

The American health care system lags well behind other sectors of the economy - and behind foreign medical systems - in adopting computers, electronic health records and information-sharing technologies that can greatly boost productivity.

There is little doubt that widespread computerization could greatly reduce the paperwork burden on doctors and hospitals, head off medication errors, and reduce the costly repetition of diagnostic tests as patients move from one doctor to another. Without an infusion of capital, the transition from paper records is not apt to happen very quickly.

Prevention

Everyone seems to be hoping that preventive medicine - like weight control, exercise, better nutrition, smoking cessation, regular checkups, aggressive screening and judicious use of drugs to reduce risks - will not only improve health but also lower costs in the long run. Preventive medicine actually costs money - somebody has to spend time counseling patients and screening them for disease - and it is not clear how soon, or even whether, substantial savings will show up. Still, the effort has to be made. The Milken Institute recently estimated that the most common chronic diseases cost the economy more than $1 trillion annually, mostly from lost worker productivity, which could balloon to nearly $6 trillion by the middle of the century.

Disease Management : Virtually all policy experts want more careful coordination of the care of chronically ill patients, who account for the largest portion of the nation's health care expenditures. Although that should improve the quality of the care they get, coordination may not cut costs as substantially as people expect. In some initial trials it has cut costs, in others not.

Drug Prices : Compared with the residents of other countries, Americans pay much more for brand-name prescription drugs, less for generic and over-the-counter drugs, and roughly the same prices for biologics. This page believes it would be beneficial to allow Medicare to negotiate with manufacturers for lower prescription drug prices and to allow cheaper drugs to be imported from abroad. The prospect for big savings is dubious.

Medical experts believe that competition is the root of the problem with U.S. health care performance. But this does not mean we advocate a state-controlled system or a single-payer system; those approaches would only make matters worse. On the contrary, competition is also the solution, but the nature of competition in health care must change. Our research shows that competition in the health care system occurs at the wrong level, over the wrong things, in the wrong geographic markets, and at the wrong time. Competition has actually been all but eliminated just where and when it is most important.

There is no villain here : Poor public-policy choices have contributed to the problem, but so have the bad choices made by health plans, hospitals, and the employers who buy their services. Decades of "reform" have failed, and attempts to reform will continue to fail until we finally get the right kind of competition working.

The health care system can achieve stunning gains in quality and efficiency. And employers, the major purchasers of health care services, could lead the transformation.

Positive-sum Competition

In a healthy system, competition at the level of diseases or treatments becomes the engine of progress and reform. Improvement feeds on itself. For that process to begin, however, the locus of competition has to shift from "Who pays?" to "Who provides the best value?" Getting there will require changes in the strategies of providers and payers and in the behaviors of employers purchasing health plans. In addition, some important system infrastructure needs to be put in place-rules and regulations that shift the incentives and create the right types of information. Let's look at each needed reform in turn.

Provider Strategies : Distinctiveness. Under positive-sum competition, providers would not attempt to match competitors' every move. Instead, they would develop clear strategies around unique expertise and tailored facilities in those areas where they can become distinctive. Most hospitals would retain a wide array of service areas, but they would not try to be all things to everyone. In most businesses, it is common sense to develop products and services that create unique value. For many hospitals, developing uniqueness is a significant change in mind-set and deciding what not to do is an even more radical idea.

No Restrictions to Choice : Under positive-sum competition, all restrictions to choice at the disease or treatment level would disappear, including network restrictions and approvals of referrals. Reasonable co-pays and large deductibles combined with medical savings accounts would let patients take some financial responsibility for their choices. But co-pays would be the same inside and outside of the network. Antitrust authorities would scrutinize system participants so that one hospital system or health plan did not unfairly dominate an important market.

Transparent Pricing : Prices would be posted and readily available. Providers would charge the same price to any patient for addressing a given medical condition, regardless of the patient's group affiliation. Providers could and would set different prices from their competitors, but that pricing would not vary simply because one patient was insured by

Aetna, another covered by Blue Cross, and another self-insured. Payers could negotiate, but price changes would have to benefit all patients, not just their own. The cost of treating a medical condition has nothing to do with who the patient's employer or insurance company is.

Price discrimination not related to costs imposes huge burdens on the system today. Having multiple prices drives up administrative costs. Patients covered by the public sector are subsidized by private-sector patients. And within the private sector, patients in large groups are subsidized by the uninsured, members of small groups, and out-of-network patients, who pay list prices. Artificially high list prices make more patients unable to pay, driving up uncompensated care expenses, which leads to ever higher list prices and bigger discounts for large groups. The price disincentives for care outside of the network stifle competition, which in turn slows quality and efficiency improvements that would otherwise benefit all patients. Without service-by-service competition, costs spiral ever higher while quality lags. The cost of dysfunctional competition far outweighs any short-term advantages system participants get from price discrimination-even for those firms that currently get the biggest discounts. [...]

Simplified Billing : A fundamental function of pricing is to convey information to consumers and competitors. Current billing practices obscure that information. Unnecessarily complex billing contributes to cost shifting, drives up administrative costs, and makes price and value comparisons virtually impossible. Under positive-sum competition, providers would have to issue a single bill for each service bundle, or for each time period in treating chronic conditions, rather than a myriad of bills for each discrete service. Many other industries have solved the problem of how to issue a single bill for customized services; among them aerospace, construction, auto repair, and consulting. A competitive health care industry could figure it out, too. Competing providers would also figure out how to give price estimates in advance of service. Such estimates would not only improve consumer choice but would also spur providers to learn about their real costs. [...]

Accessible Information : Under positive-sum competition, both the providers and the consumers of health care would get the information they need to make decisions about care. The government or a broad consortium of employers could jump-start the collection and dissemination process by agreeing on a standard set of information that would be collected nationally on a regular basis. Indeed, medical information is not unlike the corporate disclosures overseen by the SEC. The benefits of national comparisons are compelling and will unleash a tidal wave of improvements in quality and efficiency.

An obvious-and relatively uncontroversial-starting point would be to collect information on specific providers' experience with given diseases, treatments, and procedures. The data would be made publicly available after a waiting period during which providers could correct any errors. Over time, information about providers' risk-adjusted medical outcomes also would need to be collected and disseminated, allowing consumers to evaluate the providers' areas of expertise. This information would be specific to particular diseases or medical conditions, not aggregated across different areas of medical practice. A productive system would also collect or disseminate pricing information, enabling comparisons for specific treatments or procedures.

Non-discriminatory Insurance Underwriting : Two anomalies mar the pricing of health plans. First, people who are included in large risk pools (such as those who work for big companies) can get a reasonably priced health plan even if someone in the family has medical risks. But those without access to such a pool (such as people who work for small firms or are self-employed) will pay very high prices if a family member has medical risks. Realistic reform efforts need to assume that health care coverage will continue to come mostly from employers. However, risk-pooling solutions need to be developed for those who are self-employed, employed by small firms, employed part-time, or unemployed. For example, smaller companies are joining consortia for health plan purchases. For high-risk people unable to buy health plans, assigned risk pools, like those used in automobile insurance, will need to be developed.

In addition, people in small groups or with individual insurance policies face the likelihood that their premiums will rise sharply if someone in the family actually develops an expensive medical condition, even if the family has paid premiums for years without making large claims. This practice, known as "re-underwriting," negates the purpose of health insurance and must be eliminated.

Fewer Lawsuits : Malpractice litigation and the associated defensive medical practices inflict huge costs on everyone, and they have done little to raise the quality of health care. Indeed, the threat of malpractice creates incentives for physicians and hospitals to hide their mistakes rather than own up to and eliminate them. Standards for malpractice litigation need to change. Lawsuits are appropriate only in cases of truly bad medical practice, such as negligence, the use of obsolete treatments, or carelessness, not when a patient had a bad outcome despite receiving appropriate, up-to-date treatment. With better information and no restrictions on choice, many lawsuits will be averted. The money spent on enabling information and choice is an investment in removing billions of dollars of administrative and legal costs from the system.

National List of Minimum Coverage : The current system of individual negotiation and litigation over coverage is expensive. A better system would mandate a minimum level of coverage with a national list (such as the one used in the Federal Employees Health Benefits Program). Health plans could choose to cover more services and treatments for competitive reasons, but they could not be forced to do so by lawsuits. This change would refocus health care expenditures from malpractice premiums to delivery of care for more people.

Payer Strategies: Choice and Efficiency : Positive-sum competition would induce payers to compete to create value, not just to minimize cost. They would simplify billing and administrative processes. They would serve subscribers by identifying treatment alternatives and providers with excellent outcomes. They would help subscribers to know when and where it is appropriate to travel outside of their immediate areas for quality care. (Some payers have begun to post information about treatments and providers on their Web sites, but the information is often only about those treatments and providers within a small radius around the subscriber's ZIP code.) The best payers would be able to recommend effective disease-management options for subscribers with chronic conditions. Competition would shift to providing information and excellent service. Attempts to limit patients' choices or to control physicians' behavior would end.

Who Picks Up the Tab?

Pay Providers Less : With doctors dreadfully unhappy under the heavy hand of insurers, it would seem shortsighted to make them even unhappier by cutting their compensation to levels paid in other countries. But many experts believe it should be possible to tap into the vast flow of money sluicing through hospitals, nursing homes and other health care facilities to find savings.

Emphasize Primary Care : In a health system as uncoordinated as ours, many experts believe we could get better health results, possibly for less cost, if we changed reimbursement formulas and medical education programs to reward and produce more primary care doctors and fewer specialists inclined to proliferate high-cost services. It would be a long-term project.

Skin in the Game

The solution favored by many conservatives is to force consumers to shell out more money when they seek medical care so that they will think harder about whether it is really necessary. The "consumer-directed health care" movement calls for providing people with enough information about doctors and treatments so that they can make wise decisions.

There would most likely be some savings. A classic experiment by Rand researchers from 1974 to 1982 found that people who had to pay almost all of their own medical bills spent 30 percent less on health care than those whose insurance covered all their costs, with little or no difference in health outcomes. The one exception was low-income people in poor health, who went without care they needed. Any cost-sharing scheme would have to protect those unable to bear the burden.

And consumer-driven plans have limitations. Most health care spending is racked up by a small percentage of individuals whose bills are so high they are no longer subject to cost sharing; they will hardly be deterred from expensive care they desperately need. Moreover, few consumers have the competence or knowledge to second-guess a doctor's recommendations.

Single Payer

Deep in their hearts, many liberals yearn for a single-payer system, sometimes called Medicare-for-all, that would have the federal government pay for all care and dictate prices. Such a system would let the government offset the price-setting strength of the medical and pharmaceutical industries, eliminate much of the waste due to a multiplicity of private insurance plans, and greatly cut administrative costs.

But a single-payer system is no panacea for the cost

problem - witness Medicare's own cost troubles - and the approach has limited political support. Private insurers could presumably eliminate some of the waste through uniform billing and payment procedures.

By now it should be clear that there is no silver bullet to restrain soaring health care costs. A wide range of contributing factors needs to be tackled simultaneously, with no guarantee they will have a substantial impact any time soon. In many cases we do not have enough solid information to know how to cut costs without impairing quality.

So we need to get cracking on a range of solutions. The cascade of knowledge flowing from the human genome project, new nanotechnologies and the advent of treatments tailor-made for individual patients may well accelerate, not mitigate, the rise in medical spending. If we want the benefits, we will need to make them affordable.

Occasionally, scholarly studies emerge that try to explain the explosion of health care costs by identifying the various component parts of the health care system-e.g., technology, prescription drugs, hospitals, physicians, and administrative costs-in order to assess (or blame) which component is ultimately driving the increase and by how much. For example, the bipartisan Congressional Budget Office (CBO), the federal agency that estimates the fiscal impact of proposed legislation, recently published a study estimating that "about half of all growth in health care spending in the past several decades was associated with changes in medical care made possible by advances in technology."

Of course, there is certainly some truth in the notion that technological innovation, prescription drugs, new medical devices, and other innovations play a role in the rising costs. For one thing, modern medicine can do more today than it has ever done in the past. And because medicine can do more, it costs more. No one is surprised that a car in 2008 costs more than a comparable model did in 1978-even the term "comparable model" is misleading because cars today are so much better and have so many more functions, capabilities, and amenities. Nor do people seem to complain much about the fact that the new flat-screen televisions are more expensive than the older picture-tube models. Consumers know that they are getting more for their money.

We see technology and innovation affecting most areas of our lives. Yet those costs seem reasonable. Indeed, the costs usually decline shortly after a new product is bought by the "first adopters."

But maybe health care is different-something we hear often these days. Except when it isn't. Take LASIK eye surgery, for example. Doctors providing this service are constantly upgrading their expensive machines, looking for ways to attract customers and providing additional services. Still, the prices have fallen significantly since these procedures first became available. Why? The primary reason is that patients are paying out of their own pockets and demand value for their dollars.

Herein lies the fundamental economic principle that explains why health care costs are growing much faster than the rate of inflation: cost insulation. In the vast majority of cases, when a patient goes to the doctor, hospital, or pharmacy, someone else-i.e., the employer, health insurer, or government-is paying the bill. And when someone else is paying the bill, consumers have little reason to care about the costs.

While patients are complaining that they are spending more out of pocket on health care than ever before, the numbers tell a different story. According to the CBO study, consumers in 1965 were spending 52 cents out of pocket for every dollar spent on health care. That number has fallen every year, so that by 2005 they were spending only 15 cents out of every dollar.

When we as consumers are insulated from the cost of

our purchasing decisions, we tend to consume more. How much more is the subject of scholarly discussion. But many health economists think that with regard to health care, we could easily cut total spending by 20% to 30% with no ill-effects on health outcomes. Outcomes may even be better.

Employers probably know this economic fact of life better than any other segment of the population. Take business travel, for instance. When employees are traveling at company expense, they tend to be less circumspect about the price of hotel rooms, dinners, and airfares than they would if they were paying those bills themselves.

As a result, managers study travel expense forms as a check and balance to make sure that expenses are reasonable. Does anyone doubt that if employees were spending their own money on travel, they would find ways to spend less?

Similarly, employers and insurers tried to implement a checks and balances system with regard to health care expenses; managed care imposed a "manager" looking over the receipts of the patients and doctors to ensure that expenses were necessary and reasonable. And in the late 1980s through most of the 1990s, health care cost increases began to moderate. From 1994 to 1999, annual growth never exceeded 2.8%, according to the CBO study.

But there was enormous pushback from both patients and physicians, and eventually from politicians, in the form of patients' bill of rights legislation, which limited what managed care could do. As a result, the cost increases began to escalate again, leaving employers in a quandary: What should they do now?

We will never get health care costs under control until consumers have a reason to seek value-just as they do in every other sector of the economy. And the only way we're going to do that is to remove some of the cost insulation that pervades the health care system.

Consumers in most markets can compare and contrast the costs and benefits between products and services and determine for themselves whether one is providing additional value. And since they are paying for the product or service themselves, they have an economic incentive to get value for their dollars.

But in most medical care there are no prices. And for good reason: Consumers don't really care about prices because they aren't paying the bill! As a result, most medical providers have no idea what it costs them to provide a particular service, and patients who want to know can't find out.

How many Businesses could Operate like that?

But you ask: Don't other countries with government-run health care systems control their costs? Don't they spend much less than we do in the United States? Yes, but there's a reason for that: The government simply imposes from the top down how much it will spend on care. These countries aren't more efficient; the government just sets a budget. And if there isn't enough money to cover everyone's health care needs-and there never is-someone just goes without. It's called rationing, and it's rampant in those countries with government-run systems.

So how do we move to a system where patients are seeking value for their health care dollars but are still protected from the financial devastation that could come from a major accident or illness? Actually, many employers have already discovered the answer. They are shifting away from traditional health insurance to a high deductible health insurance policy, in conjunction with a Health Savings Account (HSA) or a Health Reimbursement Arrangement (HRA).

The high deductible policy costs less-often significantly less-than a traditional policy, allowing the employer to give part or all of those savings to the employee. With the HSA, for example, employers might provide a policy with a $5,000 deductible for a family, but they put $3,000 or $3,500 into a tax-free personal account that belongs to the employee. Money left over in the HSA at year's end rolls over and grows with tax-free interest. Because that money belongs to the employee, he or she has an economic incentive to ask the question that is seldom asked today: Doctor, how much will that cost? Should a major accident or illness occur, health insurance kicks in to cover those costs and protect the employee's assets.

And this approach appears to be working. Employers offering so-called consumer driven policies are seeing annual premium increases in the low single-digit range; those with traditional policies have seen average increases of 8% to 14% over the past several years.

With regard to the presidential campaign, Republican candidates have generally been supportive of removing the cost insulation by transitioning to a consumer driven model that relies on options such as HSAs or HRAs. Democrats, by contrast, have generally supported increasing the level of cost insulation, promising to ensure that everyone has comprehensive health coverage while holding down costs by imposing top-down price controls.

If health care consumers have an economic incentive to get value for their health care dollars, spending will go down. If not, then health care spending will continue growing at double-digit rates until the politicians take over and tell us how much we can spend.

4

PLANNING YOUR HEALTH CARE ADVENTURE

It takes time to establish and position your product in the international market and achieve a successful level of international sales. Your marketing strategies should be well-planned and incorporate a variety of activities that target both the international consumer and the travel trade.

Visitor medical insurance for visiting USA and Canada is very important. In the America's (USA and Canada), health care is not cheap and minor sickness can cause large medical expenses. American travel insurance, health insurance for visitors to USA is required and serious medical problems can be financially disastrous without visitor health insurance. Visitor medical Insurance or visitor visa insurance is required when you have parents or other family visiting the United States. Overseas visitor's medical insurance is required especially for immigrant communities in United States such as from India, China, UK, Bangladesh, Vietnam, Philippines, Colombia, Europe, Mexico, Australia and South America.

Visitors insurance are short-term travelers medical insurance plans for the duration of travel. These plans provide visitor insurance coverage for accident and health expenses during travel and the travelers overseas stay. Visitors Travel Insurance plans, also known as Visitors

Medical Insurance or Visitors Health insurance plans can be purchased prior to start of journey or even during the travel. Visitor insurance plans can be purchased for durations from five days to three years, and provide different medical coverages and have varying deductibles. Visitors visa insurance can be either comprehensive or have limited benefits. The cost for overseas medical insurance plans start as low as a dollar a day and vary depending on the type of health insurance for tourists in usa insurance plan.

Developing your product to an international standard requires an acute understanding of international consumer needs, motivations and different travel styles, as well as language, cultural and culinary requirements. Understanding these will enable you to see where your product fits internationally and select the right markets for your product.

Healthcare of travelers and adventurers is the specialty of Adventure Doc Clinic. Their services keep costs to a minimum by allowing several tiers of medical coverage, tailored to each group's individual needs. The medical staff of Adventure Doc is specially selected for their medical training in travel, expedition and emergency medicine. Our providers have all completed rigorous additional training to make them the most comprehensive practitioners in their fields.

The medical director of the Adventure Doc Clinic is Erik McLaughlin MD, MPH. Erik is an experienced traveler and adventurer in addition to his skills as a board certified physician. Dr. McLaughlin has completed a master's degree in international health along with his diploma in travel and tropical medicine. He is an active member of both the Wilderness Medical Society and the International Society of Travel Medicine. Erik also is a frequent instructor, lecturer and author on topics related to travel and expedition medicine.

One can buy cheap drugs online without even having to leave the place in front of your PC and get them delivered to the door of your home or office with absolute confidentiality. Break the borders and enjoy maximum discounts on the drugs. It has never been so easy to purchase such discount drugs as Alprazolam, Propecia, Adipex-P, Cialis, Xenical, Ambien CR, Wellbutrin SR, Lorcet as well as thousands of others on the Internet.

It's vital to have access to the information reflecting the real state of affairs on the pharmaceutical market since the health of a customer depends on the quality of services provided by the online pharmacy he or she shops at largely. Our resource helps a user interested in purchasing a certain medication get all the unbiased info about this or that pharmacy. We gather the information about pharmacies carefully and update our database regularly in order to guarantee its absolute reliability.

In addition to a list of pharmacies with highest customer ratings you will be offered to read honest reviews of online drugstores specializing in door-to-door delivery of prescription and non-prescription meds as well as with articles dedicated to healthcare issues and interesting health facts, which will help you to cure the specific health condition you are suffering from or dedicate more time to the prevention of it.

You can be sure that the pharmacies that make it to our listing are the most reliable sources where one can buy generic drugs as well as brand-name ones online. We help you save time, money and effort by comparing the prices, the range of provided services, payment and shipping means and the levels of reliability of various pharmacies selling pills on the Web.

PRESCRIPTION DRUGS

Looking for a perfect source of prescription drugs without a prescription and can't find anything? Indeed, it may not be as easy as it may seem to find a reliable online drugstore from India, Canada, Mexico, UK or US that would give you brand drugs or generic drugs at the same time providing guarantees of quick delivery and international shipping. Many Asian and European drugstores promise the world - but when it comes to actually keep their promises - they are not too eager anymore.

So, to make sure your shopping for FDA approved medications will always be successful and fast we have come up with a special page where you will quickly find the information you were looking for. We have done quite some work to come up with a comparison page like that and let you order drugs with no prescription needed from only most trusted places on the Internet. We looked through many places that offered to buy drugs without prescription and claimed to have cheap drugs always available.

Some of them were actually telling the truth but other ones were never to be visited by anyone whose credit card information is of any importance. We tried really hard to select only finest foreign online drugstores that would give you all the options you probably need - convenient payment options, such as money order, high quality FDA-approved discount drugs and possibility to purchase drugs with no prescription at online pharmacy that could be completely trusted. As a result of this outstanding effort you can compare best places with high quality low cost medications that have years of experience and an impressive client base.

They guarantee fast shipping and express delivery to any country in the world and offer drugs for sale round the clock! Payment methods are also very convenient and safe - they include Visa, Visa Electron, MasterCard, American Express (AmEx), Diners Club, Discover, E-Check, JCB, Debit Cards, Wire transfer and Money Transfer (Western Union and MoneyGram). Free shipping is also available - it's a bonus for customers that usually plan their shopping ahead and therefore place large orders with this drug vendor.

You can qualify as well - especially if you are looking for a medicine intended for long-term treatment. You will find lowest prices at the pharmacies we recommend you visit. The best part of this offer is - you can buy cheap drugs with no membership fees whatsoever, as we offer the information about best places to shop with for free! You will just have to pay once - at the online pharmacy you choose when placing an order. All you need to do to visit most suitable drugstore is follow the link of your choice - and best prices in the industry will be right there waiting for you!

Important Tips for Healthcare Adventure

We have compiled a great deal of packing tips after years of travelling and together with some members suggestions, we thought we should share them with other travellers setting out.

1. Security and Keeping Details Safe

Scan your passport, passport photos and paper tickets (if not the e type) in. Store this (in an email for e.g.) in your web based email account. You can also store the details of your emergency 'lost card' telephone numbers in your web based email account so you know who to contact if your credit card or ATM card is lost or stolen. This way, even if you lose everything, you have immediate access your all important information. You can even email the details page of your passport to the embassy or consulate when applying for a new one.

Also consider writing your home and destination address (and mobile number if you have one) on a self-adhesive sticky label to stick INSIDE your luggage in a visible place. If your luggage is lost and the baggage label has come off, at least the airline can still figure out whose luggage it is.

2. Split up Your Valuables

Split up your bank cards, cash, travellers' cheques and credit cards as much as possible in different pockets, your bags and wallet when packing. In case you do get robbed, at least you won't be strapped for cash (unless you have all your bags AND your wallet stolen of course!).

3. Nalgene/Small Bottles

Use nalgene/small bottles to pack toiletries and other small items. There are several sturdy and (very nearly) waterproof ones, with clear/see through ones being preferable (easier for security purposes post August 2006). You can also use small bottles to repack shampoo or lotions so that you don't have to always carry a big bottle with you. This is especially useful if you normally take these items in your carry-on luggage, which as of early 2007 is much more restricted than before.

4. Backpack Tips

When you are packing things into a backpack, place the lighter items at the bottom and the heavier ones on top. Your bag will feel lighter this way as the pack rests on your lower back. It is also smart to place the things you use the most on top. Dirty clothes are perfect to pack at the bottom of a backpack. If you are still trying to decide on the right backpack, have a look at Choosing the right Backpack on our Travel Unravelled blog.

5. Plastic Bags

It is always handy to have a few plastic bags around certain items, especially toiletries. Not only does it counter any leaking, the bags can also come in useful to keep dirty clothes in, as garbage bags or even as a makeshift umbrella. Ziplock or other airtight plastic bags are the best.

6. Pack in Plastic

Pack everything in clear plastic bags (preferably zip lock), divided into items e.g. underwear, t-shirts, shorts etc. before packing in your suitcase or backpack. One plastic bag for each type of clothing. This is extremely useful in various ways. When you unpack your bag you just take out a series of bags and you can see immediately what you want. So an overnight stay somewhere just means taking 1 item out of a bag - no rummaging!! In addition, if you have to unpack at customs etc, instead of having to disgorge all your clothing etc out in front of everybody, you can calmly take maybe 5/6 bags out, the contents of which can be clearly seen by the officials. To repack then is also dead easy. Just be sure not to leave your plastic bags lying around if you are travelling in nature! (Tip from a member)

7. Clothes

Pack only what you know you will use and if you are travelling for more than three weeks, plan to wash on the road. You can cut back on the number of clothes items by packing multi-purpose clothing, for example items that can both be worn during the day and as sleepwear.

8. Split up Clothes when Travelling with Others

When you are flying somewhere and especially if you have a few stopovers, divide the clothes between different suitcases/backpacks/bags etc. If one persons luggage doesn't arrive at the destination, they'll still have clean clothes available. Airlines generally don't compensate lost luggage for the first 24-48 hours so this will save you money if it happens to you. (Tip from a member)

9. Separate Beach Bag

When packing to head to the beach consider pre-packing whatever you might need at the beach into a beachbag inside your backpack or suitcase. Especially if travelling with kids, this will prove a timesaver!

10. Suitcase Lovers

For those using suitcases without a divider. A piece of cardboard makes an excellent divider and helps keep your clothes organized and neat as you are able to lay them out flat on the cardboard. It also makes airport inspections a lot less of a hassle as you can lift out your divider with clothes on top easily.

11. Gifts

While it is a good idea to take some small gifts with you while travelling, pre-wrapping them can be a waste of time if you are flying and your bags are opened. (Tip from a member)

12. Flashlights or Torches

When packing a flashlight or torch (or any other item with batteries for that matter), turn the batteries around so that if the item is accidentally turned on, you won't empty the batteries. Don't forget to turn the batteries back around when using the flashlight.

13. Diaper Bag

If you are travelling with babies, then the diaper bag is an excellent place to hide your valuables. This most likely will not be the first thing to be stolen. It's also a great to use as a waste bag (even when not travelling with a child!), especially at places that do not allow you to flush toilet paper. (Tip from a member)

14. Shoes

If you want to make sure everything else in your bags stays clean and odor free, place the shoes inside old socks and then inside airtight plastic bags (ziplock).

15. Carry-On

Keep any medication and important papers in your carry-on bag. On long flights with multiple stopovers (especially if flying via London, LA or other major airports), packing a fresh change of clothes is a good idea as bags tend to get delayed or lost on long haul, multiple stop flights.

You don't want to end up stuck without medication, clothes or your important papers even if it is just for a few days.

16. Roll Technique

Somehow it seems that bags will hold more if the clothes are rolled rather than folded. If you roll in tissue paper, the clothes will also get less wrinkled.

17. Travelling to Warm Destinations?

If you appreciate cold drinks think of using a six-pack cooler as a toiletry bag. Once you arrive at your destination and unload your toiletries your 'toiletry bag' guarantees cheap cold drinks on the beach, no matter how remote.

18. Local Tourism Offices

The best source of information is usually local. Check out Tourism Offices to find unbiased feedback on the best accommodation to suit your needs. Excercise caution in countries where you feel the information might not be so unbiased!

19. Minimize on Toiletries

Take only half a tube of toothpaste rolled up tight, store shampoo in small containers, only take half a roll of toilet paper (for emergencies only) and crush it so the middle is folded.

20. Take Solid Shampoo Bars and Tooth Powder

Solid shampoo bars and tooth powder (instead of tooth paste) can be easily located on the internet and make carry-on travel in this age of liquid restriction possible. Places like Beijing now bar all liquids in carry-on bags, and you'll still be able to breeze through without checking. (Tip from a member)

21. Planning on Carrying a Lot of Luggage?

While carrying a lot of luggage is not recommendable, sometimes it is necessary in the case of relocations and so on. If you have the possibility, fly via the US as airlines will allow you 64kg (two 32kg bags) instead of the 20kg in the rest of the world. Even if it is just a stopover in the US, you will be allowed to carry the extra weight. Check with your local travel agent for the details.

22. Packing List and Trip Planning

Ready to start packing? Or is there still more trip planning to be done? Check out our Packing List and Trip Planning guide to help you get the most out of your trip by planning well and packing everything.

Expedition Doctor Accompaniment

The security of having a trained and experienced physician who specializes in Travel and Expedition Medicine adds a new dimension of safety to travelers. From pre-travel consultation including preventative health care, vaccines and potential health risks to health care in the field; our doctors add comprehensive health care coverage to any group of travelers, in any destination, performing any activity.

Our physicians travel with the latest medical equipment and medications allowing them to diagnose and treat medical conditions in the field, immediately. Should illness or injury require evacuation, our doctors are there to assist and ensure the patients receive the highest level of care, regardless of location. With the help of our associated partners, medical evacuation and rescue from any location on the planet can be included in our services. This is truly a private, concierge doctor for adventurers.

Paramedic Accompaniment

Travelers and expeditions do not always have the need or budget for a private "team doctor". Adventure Doc offers paramedical services to accompany travelers and adventurers on their journeys. All paramedics have been hand-picked and benefited from additional training and experience in Travel Health and Emergency Medicine in both international and remote settings. Standard paramedical skills such as advanced life support, airway management, EKG interpretation and pain control are augmented with special training. All of our paramedics can travel with advanced medical diagnostic equipment and a medical kit containing advance life support equipment and medications, including antibiotics. Their additional training in conjunction with direct correspondence 24/7 with our medical control physician allows for a higher standard of care. Adventure Doc paramedics are capable of providing advanced medical support anywhere in the world, for any length of time and for any number of travelers/ adventurers.

Remote Provider Access (LINC system)

For travelers and adventurers looking to have the benefit of consultation 24/7 with one of our specialized healthcare providers, without the expense of actually traveling with them, our Location Independent day/Night Contact (LINC) service is ideal. This allows for direct and personal contact with our health care providers via telephone, satellite phone or internet to assist with medical advice and care. Adventure Doc can also provide these communication devices. This service allows peace of mind to discuss and start treatment of illnesses without stopping the adventure to consult a local healthcare provider. This is a 24/7 service with access to your "private health care provider".

Adventure Doc is the premier provider of health care solutions for international travelers and adventurers. All of our health care packages are highly customizable allowing us to tailor each adventure with the best medical care possible, for any required time and in any location imaginable. Please feel free to contact us for more information on how we can help you get there and back again, in good health.

To be successful in the export tourism industry, it is important to understand the roles of Inbound Tour Operators, International Wholesalers, Retail Travel Agents and other partners in the international travel distribution system. You will need to identify key partners and establish and maintain relationships with them over a long period of time. Your product price structure should also support the commission levels required by your partners in the distribution system.

Tourism Australia's Planning for Inbound Success toolkit is designed to provide you with the basic tools, knowledge and key contacts needed to enter the export tourism market. This information, combined with advice and assistance from tourism associations, industry bodies and tourism operators should put you on the path to success!

This toolkit contains advice on how to:

- Understand the travel distribution system and its rate structure;
- Research international markets to establish who will use your products;
- Recognise the different travel styles of inbound travellers;
- Develop a marketing plan to target international visitors through a range of mediums and distribution channels; and
- Seek advice from your local, regional and state tourism office.

Tourism planning in India started quite late with the first tourism policy being announced by the Government of India in November, 1982 after tourism was recognized as an industry by the Planning Commission of India in June, 1982.

In July, 1986 the Planning Commission of India set up the National Committee on Tourism in order to formulate plans for this sector. The government's initiatives of incorporating a planned tourism sector in India went a long way in boosting Indian tourism.

In May, 1992 the National Action Plan for tourism was announced. The objectives of this landmark plan for tourism planning in India were:

- To improve the economy category domestic tourism
- To develop the tourist areas socially and economically
- To preserve the environment and the national heritage
- To encourage international tourism
- To improve in world tourism India's share
- To increase opportunities for employment in this sector

India tourism planning increased with the seventh five year plan India (1985-1989). The various polices advocated by the seventh plan for tourism planning in India are:

- To promote aggressively domestic tourism
- It laid stress on creating more beach resorts
- To conduct conferences, trekking, conventions, and winter sports so that various options are available to the foreign tourists

These polices of the seventh five year plan gave a boost to the tourism planning India. To further encourage tourism planning in India, the eighth five year plan (1992- 1997) mentioned that the private sector should increase its participation in the sector. The various polices advocated by the eighth plan for tourism planning in India are:

- To develop the tourists places
- To develop winter sports, beach resort, and wildlife tourism
- To restore the projects of national heritage
- To provide in tourists centers economy class accommodation

Tourism planning in India has increased by leaps and bounds in the last few years and the government and Department of Tourism needs to make continuous efforts to ensure that tourism planning in India takes the tourism sector of the country to greater heights on a sustainable basis.

Tourism is one of many activities in a community or region that requires planning and coordination. This bulletin provides a simple structure and basic guidelines for comprehensive tourism planning at a community or regional level. Planning is the process of identifying objectives and defining and evaluating methods of achieving them. By comprehensive planning we mean planning which considers all of the tourism resources, organizations, markets, and programs within a region. Comprehensive planning also considers economic, environmental, social, and institutional aspects of tourism development.

TWO SIDES OF TOURISM PLANNING

Tourism planning has evolved from two related but distinct sets of planning philosophies and methods. On the one hand, tourism is one of many activities in an area that must be considered as part of physical, environmental, social, and economic planning. Therefore, it is common to find tourism addressed, at least partially, in a regional land use, transportation, recreation, economic development, or comprehensive plan.

The degree to which tourism is addressed in such plans depends upon the relative importance of tourism to the community or region and how sensitive the planning authority is to tourism activities.

Tourism may also be viewed as a business in which a community or region chooses to engage. Individual tourism businesses conduct a variety of planning activities including feasibility, marketing, product development, promotion, forecasting, and strategic planning. If tourism is a significant component of an area's economy or development plans, regional or community-wide marketing plans are needed to coordinate the development and marketing activities of different tourism interests in the community.

A comprehensive approach integrates a strategic marketing plan with more traditional public planning activities. This ensures a balance between serving the needs and wants of the tourists versus the needs and wants of local residents. A formal tourism plan provides a vehicle for the various interests within a community to coordinate their activities and work toward common goals. It also is a means of coordinating tourism with other community activities.

Steps in The Planning Process

Like any planning, tourism planning is goal-oriented, striving to achieve certain objectives by matching available resources and programs with the needs and wants of people. Comprehensive planning requires a systematic approach, usually involving a series of steps. The process is best viewed as an iterative and on-going one, with each step subject to modification and refinement at any stage of the planning process.

There are six steps in the planning process:

1. Define goals and objectives.
2. Identify the tourism system.
   a) Resources
   b) Organizations
   c) Markets
3. Generate alternatives.
4. Evaluate alternatives.
5. Select and implement.

6. Monitor and evaluate.

STEP ONE: Defining Goals and objectives. Obtaining clear statements of goals and objectives is difficult, but important. Ideally, tourism development goals should flow from more general community goals and objectives. It is important to understand how a tourism plan serves these broader purposes. Is the community seeking a broader tax base, increased employment opportunities, expanded recreation facilities, better educational programs, a higher quality of life? How can tourism contribute to these objectives?

If tourism is identified as a means of serving broader community goals, it makes sense to develop plans with more specific tourism development objectives. These are generally defined through a continuing process in which various groups and organizations in a community work together toward common goals. A local planning authority,chamber of commerce, visitors bureau, or similar group should assume a leadership role to develop an initial plan and obtain broad involvement of tourism interests in the community. Public support for the planning process and plan is also important.

Having a good understanding of tourism and the tourism system in your community is the first step toward defining goals and objectives for tourism development. The types of goals that are appropriate and the precision with which you are able to define them will depend upon how long your community has been involved in tourism and tourism planning.

In the early stages of tourism development, goals may involve establishing organizational structures and collecting information to better identify the tourism system in the community. Later, more precise objectives can be formulated and more specific development and marketing strategies evaluated.

STEP TWO: Identifying Your Tourism System When planning for any type of activity, it is important to first define its scope and characteristics. Be clear about exactly what your plan encompasses. A good initial question is, "What do you mean by tourism?" Tourism is defined in many ways. Generally, tourism involves people traveling outside of their community for pleasure. Definitions differ on the specifics of how far people must travel, whether or not they must stay overnight, for how long, and what exactly is included under traveling for "pleasure". Do you want your tourism plan to include day visitors, conventioneers, business travelers, people visiting friends and relatives, people passing through, or seasonal residents?

Which community resources and organizations serve tourists or could serve tourists? Generally, tourists share community resources with local residents and businesses. Many organizations serve both tourists and locals. This complicates tourism planning and argues for a clear idea of what your tourism plan entails.

You can begin to clarify the tourism system by breaking it down into three subsystems:

(1) tourism resources,

(2) tourism organizations, and

(3) tourism markets.

An initial task in developing a tourism plan is to identify, inventory, and classify the objects within each of these subsystems.

TOURISM RESOURCES are any (1) natural, (2) cultural, (3) human, or (4) capital resources that either are used or can be used to attract or serve tourists. A tourism resource inventory identifies and classifies the resources available that provide opportunities for tourism development. Conduct an objective and realistic assessment of the quality and quantity of resources you have to work with. Table I provides a suggested classification to help obtain a broad and organized picture of your tourism resources.

TOURISM ORGANIZATIONS combine resources in various proportions to provide products and services for the tourist. Table 2 is a partial list and classification of organizations that manage or coordinate tourism-related activities. It is important to recognize the diverse array of public and private organizations involved with tourism. The most difficult part of tourism planning is to get these groups to work toward common goals. You should develop a list of these organizations within your own community and obtain their input and cooperation in your tourism planning efforts. Setting up appropriate communication systems and institutional arrangements is a key part of community tourism planning.

TABLE 1. TOURISM RESOURCES

Natural Resources

* Climate-seasons
* Water resources-lakes, streams, waterfalls
* Flora-forests, flowers, shrubs, wild edibles
* Fauna-fish & wildlife
* Geological resources-topography, soils, sand dunes, beaches, caves, rocks & minerals, fossils
* Scenery-combinations of all of the above

Cultural Resources

* Historic buildings, sites
* Monuments, shrines
* Cuisine
* Ethnic cultures
* Industry, government, religion, etc.
* Anthropological resources

* Local celebrities

Human Resources

* Hospitality skills
* Management skills
* Seasonal labor force
* Performing artists-music, drama, art, storytellers, etc.
* Craftsman and artisans
* Other labor skills from chefs to lawyers to researchers
* Local populations

Capital

* Availability of capital, financing
* Infrastructure-transportation roads, airports, railroads, harbors & marinas, trails & walkways
* Infrastructure: utilities water, power, waste treatment, communications

TABLE 2. TOURISM MANAGEMENT ORGANIZATIONS AND SERVICES

Off-Site: Coordination, planning, technical assistance, research, regulation:

* Federal & state departments of commerce, transportation, & natural resources
* Federal, state, regional, & local tourism associations
* Educational organizations & consultants, e.g., Travel & Tourism Research Association; U.S. Travel Data Center; Travel Reference Center, Univ. of Colorado, Boulder; Travel, Tourism, & Recreation Resource Center, Michigan State University.
* Travel information & reservation services

On-Site: development, promotion and management, of tourism resources:

- * Federal agencies, NB. departments of commerce, transportation, & land management agencies
- * State agencies, NB. departments of commerce, transportation, & land/facility management agencies
- * Local government organizations, e.g., visitor information, chamber of commerce, convention & visitor's bureaus, parks
- * Businesses: -Accommodations: Hotels, motels, Lodges, resorts, bed & breakfast cabins & cottages, Condominiums, second homes, Campgrounds
- \- Food & Beverage: Restaurants, Grocery, Bars, nightclubs, Fast food, Catering services
- \- Transportation: Air, rail, bus; Local transportation: taxi, limo, Auto, bicycle, boat rental; Local tour services
- \- Information: Travel agencies, Information and reservation services, Automobile clubs
- \- Recreation Facilities & Services: Winter sports: ski, skating, snowmobile areas; Golf courses, miniature golf; Swimming pools, water slides, beaches; tennis, handball, racquetball courts, bowling alleys; Athletic clubs, health spas; Marinas, boat rentals and charters; hunting & fishing guides; Horseback enterprises; Sporting goods sales & rentals
- \- Entertainment: Nightclubs, amusement parks, spectator sport facilities; Gambling facilities: casinos, horse racing, bingo; video arcades; art galleries and studios, craft shops, studios, demonstrations; performing arts: theater, dance, music, film; historic & prehistoric sites; museums: art, history, science, technology; arboreta, zoos, nature centers,
- \- Special festivals and events
- \- Support services: Auto repair, gasoline service stations; boat & recreation vehicle dealers and service; retail shops: sporting goods, specialties, souvenirs, clothing; health

services: hospitals, clinics, pharmacies; laundry and dry cleaning; beauty & barber shops; babysitting services; pet care; communications: newspaper, telephone; banking and financial services

TOURISM MARKETS: Tourists makeup the third, and perhaps most important subsystem. Successful tourism programs require a strong market orientation. The needs and wants of the tourists you choose to attract and serve must be the focus of much of your marketing and development activity. Therefore, it is important to clearly understand which tourism market segments you wish to attract and serve. Tourists fall into a very diverse set of categories with quite distinct needs and wants. You should identify the different types of tourists, or market segments that you presently serve or would like to serve. This may involve one or more tourism market surveys.

A visitor survey identifies the size and nature of the existing market and asks the following questions:

* What are the primary market segments you presently attract?
* Where do they come from?
* What local businesses and facilities do they use?
* What attracted them to the community?
* How did they find out about your community?
* How satisfied are they with your offerings?

A market survey (usually a telephone survey) also can be conducted among households in regions from which you wish to attract tourists. This type of study helps identify potential markets, and means of attracting tourists to your area.

Tourism Market Segments

In a general tourism plan, some clear target tourism market segments should be identified. You might begin by defining the market area from which you will draw most of your visitors. The size of your market area depends upon the uniqueness and quality of your "product", transportation systems, tastes and preferences of surrounding populations, and your competition. Identifying the market area will help target information and promotion and define transportation routes and modes, competition, and characteristics of your market.

Next, divide your travel market into the following trip length categories:

* day trips from a 50 mile radius,
* day trips from 50 to 200 miles away,
* pass-through travelers,
* overnight trips of 1 or 2 nights (most likely weekends), and
* extended overnight vacation trips.

After you have an idea of your market area and kinds of trips you will be serving, begin defining more specific market segments like vehicle campers, downhill skiers, sightseers, family vacationers, single weekenders, and the like. These segments can be more clearly tied to particular resources, businesses, and facilities in your community.

What kinds of products and services are likely to attract each of these groups? Tourist needs as well as their impact on the local community are quite different for day tourists versus overnight tourists. Areas catering primarily to weekend traffic will experience large fluctuations in use. In deciding the relative importance of these different segments, communities need to assess both their ability to provide required services (do you have enough rooms?), as well as the demand for different types of trips relative to the supply and your competition.

THE ENVIRONMENT: A tourism plan is significantly affected by many factors in the broader environment. Indeed, one of the complexities of tourism planning is the number of variables that are outside of the control of an individual tourism business or community. These include such things as tourism offerings and prices at competing destinations, federal and state policy and legislation, currency exchange rates, the state of the economy, and weather. These factors are discussed more fully in Extension bulletin E-1959 as part of the market environment analysis.

Local populations also must be considered in tourism planning. As they compete with tourists for resources, they can be significantly affected by tourism activity, and they are an important source of support in getting tourism plans implemented. A survey of local residents can be conducted to assess community attitudes toward tourism development, identify impacts of tourism on the community, and obtain local input into tourism plans. Public hearings, workshops, and advisory boards are other ways to obtain public involvement in tourism planning. Local support and cooperation is important to the success of tourism programs and should not be overlooked.

TABLE 3. TOURISM MARKET SEGMENTS

I. Geographic market areas

II. Trip categories

Day Trips:

* short-within 50 miles
* long-up to 200 miles

Pass through traffic:

* day visitors
* overnight stays

Overnight Trips:

* weekend
* vacation

III. Activity or trip purpose

Outdoor Recreation:

* Water-based Activity:

- Boating: sail, power, cruise, row, canoe, water ski
- Swimming: pool, beach, sunbathing, scuba
- Fishing: charter, sport, from pier, boat, shore, ice

* Land-based Activity:

- Camping: backpacking, primitive, developed
- Hiking: climbing, beachcombing, spelunking
- Hunting
- Skiing: downhill, cross country
- Snowmobiling
- Bicycling
- Horseback riding
- Picnicking

* Air-based Activity:

- Airplane rides, hang gliding, ballooning, parachuting

* General:

- Nature study
- Photography or landscape painting
- Viewing natural scenery

Sightseeing & Entertainment:

* Visiting particular sites or areas:

- historic or pre-historic
- cultural
- amusements
- scenic

* Attending particular events, shows, or demonstrations:

- ethnic festivals

- sporting events
- performances
- agricultural fair or festival
- boat show
- shopping

Other Primary Purpose for Trip:

* Visiting Friends & Relatives
* Convention & Business/Pleasure

STEP THREE: Generating Alternatives. Generating alternative development and marketing options to meet your goals requires some creative thinking and brainstorming. The errors made at this stage are usually thinking too narrowly or screening out alternatives prematurely. It is wise to solicit a wide range of options from a diverse group of people. If tourism expertise is lacking in your community, seek help and advice outside the community.

Tourism planning involves a wide range of interrelated development and marketing decisions. The following development questions will get you started: * How much importance should be assigned to tourism within a community or region?

* Which general community goals is tourism development designed to serve?
* Which organization(s) will provide the leadership and coordination necessary for community tourism planning? What are the relative roles of public and private sectors?
* Segments: Which market segments should be pursued; geographic markets, trip types, activity or demographic subgroups?
* Product: What kinds of tourism products and services should be provided? Who should provide what?

* Place: Where should tourism facilities be located?
* Promotion: What kinds of promotion should be used, by whom, in which media, how much, when? What community tourism theme or image should be established?
* Price: What prices should be charged for which products and services. Who should capture the revenue?

STEP FOUR: Evaluating Alternatives. Tourism development and marketing options are evaluated by assessing the degree to which each option will be able to meet the stated goals and objectives. There are usually two parts to a systematic evaluation of tourism development and marketing alternatives: (1) Feasibility analysis, and (2) Impact assessment. These two tasks are interrelated, but think of them as trying to answer two basic questions: (1) Can it be done?, and (2) What are the consequences? A decision to take a specific action must be based both on feasibility and desirability.

FEASIBILITY ANALYSIS: First, screen alternatives and eliminate those that are not feasible due to economic, environmental, political, legal, or other factors. Evaluate the remaining set of alternatives in more detail, paying particular attention to the market potential and financial plan.

Make a realistic assessment of your community's ability to attract and serve a market segment or segments. This requires a clear understanding of the tourism market in your area and how this market is changing. Also carefully identify your competition and evaluate your advantages and disadvantages compared to the competition.

Plan toward the future because it takes time to implement decisions and for your actions to take effect. Therefore, look at the likely market and competition for several years to come. Review forecasts for the travel market in your area, if available. Careful tracking of tourism trends in your own community can help identify changes in the market that you will have to adapt to.

IMPACT ASSESSMENT: When evaluating alternative development and marketing strategies it is important to understand the impacts, both positive and negative, of proposed actions. Table 4 presents a classification of economic, environmental, and social impacts associated with tourism development. The types of impacts and their importance vary across different communities and proposed actions. Generally, the size, extent, and nature of tourism impacts depend upon:

* volume of tourist activity relative to local activity
* length and nature of tourist contacts with the community
* degree of concentration/dispersal of tourist activity in the area
* similarities or differences between local populations and tourists
* stability/sensitivity of local economy, environment, and social structure
* how well tourism is planned, controlled, and managed.

Look at both the benefits and costs of any proposed actions. While tourism development can increase income, revenues, and employment, it also involves costs. Evaluate benefits and costs of tourism development from the perspectives of local government, businesses, and residents.

TABLE 4. IMPACTS OF TOURISM

Economic Impacts:

* Sales, revenue, and income
* Employment
* Fiscal impact-taxes, infrastructure costs
* Prices

* Economic base & structure

Environmental Impacts:

* Lands
* Waters
* Air
* Infrastructure
* Flora & fauna

Social Impacts:

* Population structure & distribution
* Values & attitudes
* Education
* Occupations
* Safety & security
* Congestion & crowding
* Community spirit & cohesion
* Quality of life

Impacts on Local Government

Local government provides most of the infrastructure and many of the services essential to tourism development, including highways, public parks, law enforcement, water and sewer, garbage collection and disposal. Evaluate tourism decisions with a clear understanding of the capacity of the local infrastructure and services relative to anticipated needs, and take into account both the needs of local populations and tourists.

A fiscal impact analysis evaluates the impact of tourism on the community's tax base and local government costs. It entails predicting the additional infrastructure and service requirements of tourism development, estimating their costs, deciding who will pay for/provide them, and how. Will tourism generate increased local government revenue through fees and charges, local sales or use taxes, increased property values or property tax rates, or larger local shares of federal and state tax revenues?

Impacts on Business and Industry

Businesses that are directly serving tourists benefit from sales to tourists. Through secondary impacts, tourism activity also benefits a wide range of businesses in a community. For example, a local textile industry may sell to a linen supply firm that serves hotels and motels catering primarily to tourists. A local forest products industry sells to a lumberyard where local woodcarvers or furniture makers buy their supplies. They in turn sell to tourists through various retail outlets. All of these businesses benefit from tourism.

If most products and services for tourists are bought outside of the local area, much of the tourist spending "leaks" out of the local economy. The more a community is "self-sufficient" in serving tourists, the larger the local impact.

Impacts on Residents

Local residents may experience a broad range of both positive and negative impacts from tourism development. Tourism development may provide increased employment and income for the community. Although tourism jobs are primarily in the service sectors and are often seasonal, part time, and low-paying, these characteristics, are neither universal nor always undesirable. Residents may value opportunities for part time and seasonal work. In particular, employment opportunities and work experiences for students or retirees may be desired.

Residents may also benefit from local services that otherwise would not be available. Tourism development may mean a wider variety of retailers and restaurants, or a better community library. It may also mean more traffic, higher prices, and increases in property values and local taxes. The general quality of the environment and life in the community may go up or down due to tourism development. This depends on the nature of tourism development, the preferences and desires of local residents, and how well tourism is planned and managed.

STEPS FIVE AND SIX: Implementation, and Monitoring and Evaluation. We will not attempt a complete discussion of decisionmaking, plan implementation, and monitoring, but these are critical steps in the success of a tourism plan. A set of specific actions should be prescribed with clearly defined responsibilities and timetables. Monitor progress in implementing the plan and evaluate the success of the plan in meeting its goals and objectives on a regular basis. Plans generally need to be adjusted over time due to changing goals, changing market conditions, and unanticipated impacts. It is a good idea to build monitoring and evaluation systems into your planning efforts.

CONCLUDING REMARKS : Successful tourism planning and development means serving both tourists and local residents. The bulletins in this series stress the importance of a market orientation for attracting and serving tourists. This market orientation must be balanced with a clear view of how tourism serves the broader community interest and an understanding of the positive and negative impacts of tourism development.

Remember, tourism should serve the community first and the tourist second. Tourism development must be compatible with other activities in the area and be supported by the local population. Therefore, the tourism plan should be closely coordinated with other local and regional planning efforts, if not an integral part of them.

Philosophy of Healthcare

The philosophy of healthcare is the study of the ethics, processes, and people which constitute the maintenance of health for human beings. For the most part, however, the philosophy of healthcare is best approached as an indelible component of human social structures. That is, the societal institution of healthcare can be seen as a necessary phenomenon of human civilization whereby an individual continually seeks to improve, mend, and alter the overall nature and quality of his or her life.

The philosophy of healthcare is primarily concerned with the following elemental questions:

- Who requires and/or deserves healthcare? Is healthcare a fundamental right of all people?
- What should be the basis for calculating the cost of treatments, hospital stays, drugs, etc.?
- How can healthcare best be administered to the greatest number of people?
- What are the necessary parameters for clinical trials and quality assurance?
- Who, if anybody, can decide when a patient is in need of "comfort measures" (euthanasia)?

However, the most important question of all is 'what is health?'. Unless this question is addressed any debate about healthcare will be vague and unbounded. For example, what exactly is a health care intervention? What differentiates healthcare from engineering or teaching, for example? Is health care about 'creating autonomy' or acting in people's best interests? Or is it always both? A 'philosophy' of anything requires baseline philosophical questions, as asked, for example, by the philosopher Professor David Seedhouse.

Ultimately, the purpose, objective, and meaning of healthcare philosophy is to consolidate the abundance of information regarding the ever-changing fields of biotechnology, medicine, and nursing. And seeing that healthcare typically ranks as one of the largest spending areas of governmental budgets, it becomes important to gain a greater understanding of healthcare as not only a social institution, but also as a political one. In addition, healthcare philosophy attempts to highlight the primary movers of healthcare systems; be it nurses, doctors, allied health professionals, hospital administrators, health insurance companies (HMOs and PPOs), the government (Medicare and Medicaid), and lastly, the patients themselves.

The ethical and moral premises of healthcare are convoluted and numerous. In order to consolidate such an enormous field of ethical thought, it becomes necessary to focus on what makes healthcare ethics truly different from other forms of morality. And on the whole, it can be said that healthcare itself is a "special" institution within society. With that said, healthcare ought to "be treated differently from other social goods" in a society. It is an institution of which we are all a part whether we like it or not. At some point in every person's life, a decision has to be made regarding one's healthcare. Can he/she afford it? Does he/she deserve it? Does he/she need it?

Where should he/she go to get it? Does he/she even want it? And it is this last question which poses the biggest dilemma facing a person. After weighing all of the costs and benefits of her healthcare situation, the person has to decide if the costs of healthcare outweigh the benefits. More than basic economic issues are at stake in this conundrum. In fact, a person must decide whether or not his/her life is ending or if it is worth salvaging. Of course, in instances where the patient is unable to decide due to medical complications, like a coma, then the decision must come from elsewhere. And defining that "elsewhere" has proven to be a very difficult endeavor in healthcare philosophy.

Medical Ethics

Whereas bioethics tends to deal with more broadly-based issues like the consecrated nature of the human body and the roles of science and technology in healthcare, medical ethics is specifically focused on applying ethical principals to the field of medicine. It is a large and relatively new area of study in ethics.

And one of the major premises of medical ethics surrounds "the development of valuational measures of outcomes of health care treatments and programs; these outcome measures are designed to guide health policy and so must be able to be applied to substantial numbers of people, including across or even between whole societies." Terms like beneficence and non-maleficence are vital to the overall understanding of medical ethics. Therefore, it becomes important to acquire a basic grasp of the varying dynamics that go into a doctor-patient relationship.

Nursing Ethics

Like medical ethics, nursing ethics is very narrow in its focus, especially when compared to the expansive field of bioethics. For the most part, "nursing ethics can be defined as having a two-pronged meaning," whereby it is "the examination of all kinds of ethical and bioethical issues from the perspective of nursing theory and practice." This definition, although quite vague, centers on the practical and theoretical approaches to nursing. The American Nurses Association (ANA) endorses an ethical code that emphasizes "values" and "evaluative judgments" in all areas of the nursing profession. And since moral issues are extremely prevalent throughout nursing, it is important to be able to recognize and critically respond to situations that warrant and/or necessitate an ethical decision.

Business Ethics

Balancing the cost of care with the quality of care is a major issue in healthcare philosophy. In Canada and some parts of Europe, democratic governments play a major role in determining how much public money from taxation should be directed towards the healthcare process. In the United States and other parts of Europe, private health insurance corporations as well as government agencies are the agents in this precarious life-and-death balancing act. According to medical ethicist Leonard J. Weber, "Good-quality healthcare means cost-effective healthcare," but "more expensive healthcare does not mean higher-quality healthcare" and "certain minimum standards of quality must be met for all patients" regardless of health insurance status.

This statement undoubtedly reflects the varying thought processes going into the bigger picture of a healthcare cost-benefit analysis. In order to streamline this tedious process, health maintenance organizations (HMOs) like BlueCross BlueShield employ large numbers of actuaries (colloquially known as "insurance adjusters") to ascertain the appropriate balance between cost, quality, and necessity in a patient's healthcare plan. A general rule in the health insurance industry is as follows:

The least costly treatment should be provided unless there is substantial evidence that a more costly intervention is likely to yield a superior outcome. This generalized rule for healthcare institutions "is perhaps one of the best expressions of the practical meaning of stewardship of resources," especially since "the burden of proof is on justifying the more expensive intervention, not the less expensive one, when different acceptable treatment options exist."

POLITICS IN HEALTH CARE

Much has been said with regard to the political philosophy of healthcare. The debate surrounding universal health care and private health care is particularly potent in the United States. The 1960s however saw a plethora of concrete moves by the federal government to consolidate and modernize the U.S. healthcare system. With Lyndon Johnson's Great Society initiative, the U.S. established public health insurance for both senior citizens and the underprivileged. Known as Medicare and Medicaid, these two healthcare programs granted certain groups of Americans access to adequate healthcare services. Although these healthcare programs were a giant step in the direction of socialized medicine, many people think that the U.S. needs to do more for its citizenry with respect to healthcare coverage. Opponents of universal health care see it as a dumbing down of the healthcare quality that already exists in the United States.

Patients' Bill of Rights

In 2001, the federal government of the United States undertook an initiative to provide patients with an explicit list of rights concerning their healthcare. This initiative was essentially taking some of ideas found in the Consumers' Bill of Rights and applying it to the field of healthcare. It was undertaken in an effort to ensure the quality of care of all patients by preserving the integrity of the processes that occur in the healthcare industry.

Standardizing the nature of healthcare institutions in this manner proved rather provocative. In fact, many interest groups, including the American Medical Association (AMA) and Big Pharma came out vehemently against the congressional bill. Basically, providing emergency medical care to anyone, regardless of health insurance status, as well as the right of a patient to hold their health plan accountable for any and all harm done proved to be the biggest stumbling blocks for this bill. As a result of this intense opposition, the initiative eventually failed to pass Congress in 2002.

RESEARCH AND SCHOLARSHIP

Considering the rapid pace at which the fields of medicine and health science are developing, it becomes important to investigate the most proper and/or efficient methodologies for conducting research. On the whole, "the primary concern of the researcher must always be the phenomenon, from which th research question is derived, and only subsequent to this can decisions be made as to the most appropriate research methodology, design, and methods to fulfill the purposes of the research." This statement on research methodology places the researcher at the forefront of his findings.

That is, the researcher becomes the person who makes or breaks his or her scientific inquiries rather than the research itself. Even so, "interpretive research and scholarship are creative processes, and methods and methodology are not always singular, a priori, fixed and unchanging." Therefore, viewpoints on scientific inquiries into healthcare matters "will continue to grow and develop with the creativity and insight of interpretive researchers, as they consider emerging ways of investigating the complex social world."

Clinical Trials

Clinical trials are a means through which the healthcare industry tests a new drug, treatment, or medical device. The traditional methodology behind clinical trials consists of various phases in which the emerging product undergoes a series of intense tests, most of which tend to occur on interested and/or compliant patients. The U.S. government has an established network for tackling the emergence of new products in the healthcare industry.

The Food and Drug Administration (FDA) typically conducts appropriate trials on new drugs coming from pharmaceutical companies. Along with the FDA, the National Institutes of Health sets the guidelines for all kinds of clinical trials relating to infectious diseases. For cancer, the National Cancer Institute (NCI) sponsors a series or cooperative groups like CALGB and COG in order to standardize protocols for cancer treatment.

Quality Assurance

The primary purpose of quality assurance (QA) in healthcare is to ensure that the quality of patient care is in accordance with established guidelines. The government usually plays a significant role in providing structured guidance for treating a particular disease or ailment. However, protocols for treatment can also be worked out at individual healthcare institutions like hospitals and HMOs.

In some cases, quality assurance is seen as a superfluous endeavor, as many healthcare-based QA organizations, like QARC, are publicly funded at the hands of taxpayers. However, many people would agree that healthcare quality assurance, particularly in the areas cancer treatment and disease control are necessary components to the vitality of any legitimate healthcare system. With respect to quality assurance in cancer treatment scenarios, the Quality Assurance Review Center (QARC) is just one example of a QA facility that seeks "to improve the standards of care" for patients "by improving the quality of clinical trials medicine."

Everybody who wishes to have a child wants it to be perfect (at least at birth). Nobody wants and/or wishes for their child to be born with Down Syndrome or Cerebral Palsy. In fact, obstetricians have the most medical malpractice lawsuits filed against them. As a result, they have to pay the highest premiums for malpractice insurance. These high costs inevitably become a hindrance not only to the doctors, but also to the healthcare industry as a whole. And although patients and their families have the right to appeal and confront a physician regarding the quality of treatment received, there must be a limit as to how far they can go. Frivolous lawsuits are clearly becoming a major problem for healthcare providers.

The ecophilosophy of Garrett Hardin constitutes one perspective from which to view the reproductive rights of human beings. For the most part, Hardin argues that it is immoral to have large families, especially since it does a disservice to society in the sense that there is only a finite number of resources in the world. In an essay entitled The Tragedy of the Commons, Hardin states,

To couple the concept of freedom to breed with the belief that everyone born has an equal right to the commons is to lock the world into a tragic course of action.

This statement essentially summarizes Hardin's major point concerning the negligible right of all human beings to procreate. Moreover, Hardin is a vocal critic of the United Nations' Universal Declaration of Human Rights (UDHR), which states that "any choice and decision with regard to the size of the family must irrevocably rest with the family itself, and cannot be made by anyone else."

As for healthcare philosophy, Hardin's ecophilosophical views may seem like a stretch. Nevertheless, they are important to keep in mind, especially when considering the call for healthcare as a universal birth right of all people. The increasing strains placed on healthcare systems are primarily the result of a growing human population. One way of mitigating healthcare costs is to moderate population growth. The fewer people there are to take care of, the less expensive healthcare will become. And to apply this logic to what medical ethicist Leonard J. Weber previously suggested, less expensive healthcare does not necessarily mean poorer quality healthcare.

Birth and Living

The concept of being "well-born" is not new. On the whole, it takes on a fairly racist undertone. The Nazis practiced eugenics in order to cleanse the gene pool of what were perceived to be unwanted or harmful elements.

This "race hygiene movement in Germany evolved from a theory of Social Darwinism, which had become popular throughout Europe" and the United States during the 1930s. A German phrase that embodies the whole nature of this practice is lebensunwertes Leben or "life unworthy of life."

In connection with healthcare philosophy, the theory of natural rights becomes a rather pertinent subject. After birth, man is effectively endowed with a series of natural rights that cannot be banished under any circumstances. One major proponent of natural rights theory was seventeenth-century English political philosopher John Locke. With regard to the natural rights of man, Locke states,

If God's purpose for me on earth is my survival and that of my species, and the means to that survival are my life, health, liberty and property - then clearly I don't want anyone to violate my rights to these things.

Although partially informed by his religious understanding of the world, Locke's statement can essentially be viewed as an affirmation of the right to preserve one's life at all costs. This point is precisely where healthcare as a human right becomes relevant.

The process of preserving and maintaining one's health throughout life is a matter of grave concern. Once alive, how should people exercise their natural right to preserve their life through good health? At some point in every person's life, his or her health is going to decline regardless of all measures taken to prevent such a collapse. Coping with this inevitable decline can prove quite problematic for some people. For Enlightenment philosopher René Descartes, the depressing and gerontological implications of aging pushed him to believe in the prospects of immortality through a wholesome faith in the possibilities of reason.

Basic Human Rights

One of the most basic human rights is the right to live, and thus, preserve one's life. But what about the right to die, and thus, end one's life? Needless to say, this is a very controversial topic. Often, religious values of varying traditions tend to seep into the picture in one fashion or another. Terms like "mercy killing" and "assisted suicide" are frequently used to describe this process. Proponents of euthanasia claim that it is particularly necessary for patients suffering from a terminal illness. However, opponents of a self-chosen death purport that it is not only immoral, but wholly against the pillars of reason.

In a certain philosophical context, death can be seen as the ultimate existential moment in one's life. Death is the deepest cause of a primordial anxiety (Die Anfechtung) in a person's life. And it is in this emotional state of anxiety that "the Nothing" is revealed to the person. According to twentieth-century German existentialist/phenomenologist philosopher Martin Heidegger,

The Nothing is the complete negation of the totality of beings. And thus, for Heidegger, humans finds themselves in a very precarious and fragile situation (constantly hanging over the abyss) in this world. This concept can be simplified to the point where at bottom, all that a person has in this world is his or her Being. And no matter how individuals proceed in life, their existence will always be marked by finitude and solitude.

The prospect or self-realization that one's life is about to end is quite frightening to say the least. But why is this the case? When considering near-death experiences, humans feels this primordial anxiety overcome them. It robs them of speech and thought, but not feeling. Therefore, it is important for healthcare providers to recognize the onset of this entrenched despair in patients who are nearing their respective deaths.

Another philosophical inquiry into death centers on the heavy reliance on science and technology in the healthcare profession. This reliance is especially evident in Westernized medicine, as it is difficult to make apt connections to primitive means of healthcare in the developing world. Even so, Heidegger makes a rather fascinating allusion to this reliance in what he calls the allure or "character of exactness." In effect, man is inherently attached to "exactness" because it gives him a sense of purpose or reason in a world that is largely defined by what appears to be chaos and irrationality. And as the moment of death is approaching, a moment marked by utter confusion and fear, he tries to locate a sense of meaning and purpose behind it all.

Aside from the role that science and technology plays in death, palliative care constitutes a specialized area of healthcare philosophy that specifically relates to patients who are terminally ill. Similar to hospice, this area of healthcare philosophy is becoming increasingly important as more patients are preferring to receive healthcare services in their homes. Even though the terms "palliative" and "hospice" are typically used in an interchangeable fashion, they are actually quite different. And the major difference resides in the fact that hospice care is a benefit associated with Medicare while palliative care is not.

As a patient nears the end of his life, it is more comforting to be in a private home-like setting instead of a hospital. Palliative care has generally been reserved for those who have a terminal illness. However, it is now being applied to patients in all kinds of medical situations, including chronic fatigue and other bothersome symptoms.

Role Development

The manner in which nurses, physicians, patients, and administrators interact is crucial for the overall efficacy of a healthcare system. From the viewpoint of the patients, healthcare providers can be seen as being in a privileged position, whereby they have the power to alter the patients' quality of life. And yet, there are strict divisions among healthcare providers that can sometimes lead to an overall decline in the quality of patient care. When nurses and physicians are not on the same page with respect to a particular patient, a compromising situation may arise. Effects stemming from a "gender gap" between nurses and doctors are detrimental to the professional environment of a hospital workspace.

5

TREATMENT COST

Health Tourism is broadly defined as 'Cost-Effective' private medical care in collaboration with the Tourism Industry for overseas patients needing specialized treatment. With globalization increased number of people are travelling to another countries to get treated abroad, here quality is the primary factor however cost involved in obtaining quality health care attention that could be surgical or non-surgical procedures is another most important determining factor.

The advantages of medical tourism are many. Travelling to India allows the medical tourist to access high quality medical care at much lower prices than in the UK. It also avoids long waiting times for surgery and other treatments and potentially allows patients to obtain procedures not available in the UK. Medical tourists find that the cost of their treatment (including the return airfare, holiday and accommodation) leaves them with a total bill substantially less than they would have spent just on having the procedure in the UK.

India is an obvious choice for safe and cost-effective medical treatment and despite any prejudices about healthcare in developing countries India's private hospitals have earned their reputation as world-class institutions with state-of-the-art technology and highly skilled medical personnel. Indian doctors are considered to be among the best in the world and their high level of surgical expertise evolves from many years of training. Many doctors train and work in the US, Europe or the UK after completing their studies in India.

India has a number of corporate hospitals, many of which are gaining ISO9001 standardisation status (the voluntary standardisation run by a non governmental body where hospitals must pass rigorous tests to be certified). The Indian government is also establishing minimum quality standards to reassure patients seeking treatment abroad and the Joint Commission International USA is the Gold Standard accreditation for US and European hospitals which represents the highest levels of patient care and patient safety.

With attractively low prices in comparison with the West and some of the most cost-effective healthcare facilities in the world India's healthcare industry is booming as patients choose the East to undergo heart surgery, knee transplant surgery, cosmetic surgery and dentistry and reap great savings in the process. Medical tourism 'packages' often include transfers, accommodation, sight-seeing and/or a relaxing post-operative trip with the added benefits of India's legacy of health-inducing therapies like Ayurveda, yoga or meditation thrown in.

Constraints such as high costs and long waiting lists for treatment or surgery have prompted people to look at effective options. Developing countries, significantly India is turning out to be a favorite health treatment destination among people in developed countries like US, UK, etc. as India offers high quality treatment at fractional costs with minimal waiting period.

Healthcare and tourism may seem contradictory but people have been traveling to distant lands for rejuvenation packages. The effort now is to institutionalize and re-route patients to Indian hospitals for Medical Treatment for all kind of healthcare areas to the extent of super specialty fields in the medical science.

According to the report, "higher prices for health services such as prescription drugs, hospital stays, and doctor visits, are the main reason for higher U.S. spending. The latest data from the Organization for Economic Cooperation and Development (OECD), which compare trends among 30 industrialized countries, show that the U.S. spent $5,267 per capita on health care in 2002-53 percent more than any other country." And that "other country" is Switzerland, which has the distinction of being the only other OECD nation that spends more than 10% of GDP on health care. When compared to the median expenditure, US costs are much higher.

Medical tourism is becoming more popular with prices for treatment abroad becoming highly attractive for UK patients. In 2006, we carried out the Treatment Abroad PriceWatch survey to quantify the differences in costs of elective surgery, cosmetic surgery and dental procedures performed abroad compared to the UK, and highlight the savings that can be made. The survey carried out by European Research Specialists Ltd compiled data from 108 clinics, hospitals and healthcare providers in 30 countries, roughly a third of the estimated number of overseas hospitals and clinics promoting their services to the UK market. The price comparisons for surgical treatments take into account hospital and doctor charges as well as typical flights and hotel bills for the expected length of stay.

The cost of merely having a small white filling or a tooth capped in a private dentist centre in the UK doesn't leave much change out of a £50 note, but you can get much more value for money in India without skimping on quality. In India expect to save over 70% on cosmetic dentistry treatments such as dental implants, which typically cost £1,500 in the UK, and only £500 in India.

Access and Waiting Lists

One of the metronomic chants used by those disparaging other nations' health care systems is the much-hated "waiting list" - with the assumption that their costs are lower because people have to wait forever for a liver, dialysis, blood test, or MRI. The facts tell a different story:

"Despite the lack of waiting lists, Americans do not have access to a greater supply of health care resources than people in most other OECD countries. In fact, the U.S. has fewer per capita hospital beds, physicians, nurses, and CT scanners than the OECD median." The report also compared costs in nations with waiting lists for certain procedures to those without - surprisingly, those with waiting lists actually had higher costs. I don't know if they had waiting lists as a means of addressing higher costs, or somehow the lists drove costs higher. I am also curious as to the mix of generalists to specialists...

Malpractice and Defensive Medicine

Yes, the US has more malpractice suits per capita than other nations (twice as many as in the UK and Australia, and 3.5 times more than in Canada). But, and here's the big "but", the average award in the US was 14% lower than in Canada, 36% less than the average in the UK, and slightly higher than Australia's average expense (the other countries studied for this factor). So, while our "frequency" is higher, our "severity" (cost per claim) is lower.

Notably, the total impact of malpractice expenses as a percentage of US health care costs was less than 0.5%. That does not factor in defensive medicine - but even the highest estimate of the excess costs resulting from defensive medicine adds but 9% to our total costs - not enough to explain the difference in total costs between the US and other OECD countries.

Price

Here's the issue, at least according to this report. We pay more for "prescription drugs, hospital stays, and doctor visits" than other industrialized nations.

Cautionary note -although it is clear that malpractice, defensive medicine, and too many CT scanners and hospital beds are likely not significant contributors to the vast gap in costs between the US and other countries, the report does not indicate what factors are driving prices.

Remember that this compares the US to other countries; cost drivers that impact you, your business, and your premiums must be examined through the lens of US experience. Price is driving your costs, but it's impact is multiplied by utilization and frequency.

Huge savings can be made in India on general and specialist surgery. In the UK, the typical waiting time on the NHS for a cardiac-by-pass is ten months and to have this operation done privately it would cost between £14,000 and 17,000. However, in India the cost is £3,750, which, even with flights and accommodation on top, is over one third cheaper).

It can take up to 11 months on the NHS to get a hip replacement and privately this would cost between £9,000 and £13,000. Compare this with India where you can expect to pay just £3,600* for the treatment done privately.

Regarding cosmetic surgery Rhinoplasty (a nose reshape) costs between £3,500 to £5,000 in the UK compared to £1,100 up to £1,500 in India. As for private dentistry, just having one tooth capped in the UK can cost as much as £45, but in India having your whole set of teeth capped costs just £400.

MEDICAL DEBT

It refers to debt incurred by individuals due to health care costs and related expenses.Medical debt is different from other forms of debt, because it is usually incurred accidentally or faultlessly. People do not plan to fall ill or hurt themselves, and health care remedies are often unavoidable; medical debt is often treated with more sympathy than other kinds of debt resulting in advice that people ought not try to convert it to credit card debt.

Medical debt is an especially notable phenomenon in the United States - the US being the world's only developed country not to offer universal health care. In less developed nations those on low income in need of treatment will often avail themselves of what ever help they can from either the state or NGOs without going into debt, but in the US medical debt has been found by a 2009 study to be the primary cause of personal bankruptcy.

A 2007 survey had found about 70 million Americans either have difficulty paying for medical treatment or have medical debt. Studies have found people are most likely to accumulate large medical debts when they do not have health insurance to cover the costs of necessary medications, treatments, or procedures - in 2009 about 50 million Americans have no health coverage. However, about 60% of those found to have medical debt were insured.

Health insurance plans rarely cover any and all health-related expenses; for insured people, the gap between insurance coverage and the affordability of health care manifests as medical debt. As with any type of debt, medical debt can lead to an array of personal and financial problems - including having to go without food and heat plus a reluctance to seek further medical treatment. Aggressive debt collecting has been highlighted as an aggravating factor. A study has found about 63% of adults with medical debt avoided further medical treatment, compared with only 19% of adults who had no such debt.

Five Tips To Lower Costs Of Dental Treatment

The threat of high billing at the dentists in the U.S. is always there in more than half of the residents, mainly due to the fact that they lack dental insurance.

But having dental insurance is not enough to cut all the costs. A few dental treatments charge 50% of the cost even to those with the insurance.

One other limitation with the dental insurance plans is that many companies impose a limit on the covers per year, like around $1500 each year, and some high cost dental procedures like implants are not covered by the Insurance companies.

Here are some thoughts in people's minds, and how they can save money on dental treatments.

1. Can I ask for more Negotiation on the Dentist Bills?

Negotiations are always to be counted, no matter how small or big they are. If you are already on an dental insurance plan, you can't expect more negotiation on the price as the dentist is already taking off around 15-20% of the cost of the treatment.

If you are not on any dentL insurance plan, you can try wiggling around with the price before the treatment starts, as the dentist too is aware of losing something in the business if you knock the adjacent door, taking the cost into consideration.

According to Californian company which evaluates the dental insurance plans coverage, most of the dentists in the U.S. reduce the cost of treatment by around 5% when the patient agrees to pay the entire cost upfront. The patients have the right to ask for a discount that the insured patients are given, and since the recession drop, the patient count has never rose as most of them had lost the insurance coverage they were with.

2. Are there any Affordable Dental Treatment Options for Uninsured People?

There are a few options through which the uninsured dental patients can get some reduction on the cost of dentistry treatment, one of which includes the dental plans provided by the dentists themselves without involving any government services etc. and here they charge monthly or quarterly premiums to the patients. The dentists also sometimes connect the patients to third party payment systems, which take care of the discounts and payment issues.

Some insurance companies and dentists, just to keep the patients flow towards them, offer some discount cards for free or with a very low premium.

3. Do Dental Students Providing Care for less in Dental Schools?

The treatments like root canal therapy, dental extractions, teeth cleaning etc. are done by the students who are being trained at the dental schools, all under the supervision of the qualified dentists, but the charge for the dental treatments become less and nearly half in schools like The Indiana University School of Dentistry, as these treatments are done by students in a slower rate.

The qualified dentists in their private clinics do the same treatment by consuming lesser time, and so the cost of treatment is high.

Still, the breaks in prices are dependent on the type of dental treatment. For example, the cut down of cost for orthodontic treatments is not as high as that done for the regular treatment options. Are there any other options for saving money on dental care?

4. Dental Tourism

Dental tourism plays a very important role when it comes to saving money on major treatment procedures, like the orthodontic or surgical stuff. The overseas dental care costs a fraction of the cost in U.S., but the patient needs to keep in mind about the travel costs, the time being spent for traveling and they need to tackle any other issues during the travel.

According to U.S. dentists, anyone who is considering traveling abroad should first search for any recommendations, and if possible, they need to search for dentists who are qualified from the U.S. so that they comply with the terms that apply in the U.S. and overseas too.

5. Barter Your Services to Dental Treatment

Patients with skills on different stuffs that can help the dentists can take the advantage of it and barter their services with the cost of treatment that the dentist does. One of the most common example here is the designing of web pages for the dentists, providing an online exposure for them, in exchange to the treatment costs.

Health Economics

Health economics is a branch of economics concerned with issues related to scarcity in the allocation of health and health care. In broad terms, health economists study the functioning of the health care system and the private and social causes of health-affecting behaviors such as smoking.

A seminal 1963 article by Kenneth Arrow, often credited with giving rise to the health economics as a discipline, drew conceptual distinctions between health and other goals. Factors that distinguish health economics from other areas include extensive government intervention, intractable uncertainty in several dimensions, asymmetric information, and externalities.

Governments tend to regulate the health care industry heavily and also tend to be the largest payer within the market. Uncertainty is intrinsic to health, both in patient outcomes and financial concerns. The knowledge gap that exists between a physician and a patient creates a situation of distinct advantage for the physician, which is called asymmetric information.

Externalities arise frequently when considering health and health care, notably in the context of infectious disease. For example, making an effort to avoid catching the common cold affects people other than the decision maker.

The scope of health economics is neatly encapsulated by Alan Williams' "plumbing diagram" dividing the discipline into eight distinct topics:

- What influences health? (other than health care)
- What is health and what is its value
- The demand for health care
- The supply of health care
- Micro-economic evaluation at treatment level
- Market equilibrium
- Evaluation at whole system level; and,
- Planning, budgeting and monitoring mechanisms.

HEALTH CARE DEMAND

The demand for health care is a derived demand from the demand for health. Health care is demanded as a means for consumers to achieve a larger stock of "health capital." The demand for health is unlike most other goods because individuals allocate resources in order to both consume and produce health.

The above description gives three roles of persons in health economics. The World Health Report (p. 52) states that people take four roles in the health care: 1. Contributors 2. Citizens (stewardship) 3. Providers 4. Consumers

Michael Grossman's 1972 model of health production has been extremely influential in this field of study and has several unique elements that make it notable. Grossman's model views each individual as both a producer and a consumer of health. Health is treated as a stock which degrades over time in the absence of "investments" in health, so that health is viewed as a sort of capital.

The model acknowledges that health care is both a consumption good that yields direct satisfaction and utility, and an investment good, which yields satisfaction to consumers indirectly through increased productivity, fewer sick days, and higher wages. Investment in health is costly as consumers must trade off time and resources devoted to health, such as exercising at a local gym, against other goals. These factors are used to determine the optimal level of health that an individual will demand.

The model makes predictions over the effects of changes in prices of health care and other goods, labour market outcomes such as employment and wages, and technological changes. These predictions and other predictions from models extending Grossman's 1972 paper form the basis of much of the econometric research conducted by health economists.

In Grossman's model, the optimal level of investment in health occurs where the marginal cost of health capital is equal to the marginal benefit. With the passing of time, health depreciates at some rate ?. The interest rate faced by the consumer is denoted by r. The marginal cost of health capital can be found by adding these variables: . The marginal benefit of health capital is the rate of return from this capital in both market and non-market sectors.

In this model, the optimal health stock can be impacted by factors like age, wages and education. As an example, increases with age, so it becomes more and more costly to attain the same level of health capital or health stock as one ages. Age also decreases the marginal benefit of health stock. The optimal health stock will therefore decrease as one ages.

Beyond issues of the fundamental, "real" demand for medical care derived from the desire to have good health (and thus influenced by the production function for health) is the important distinction between the "marginal benefit" of medical care (which is always associated with this "real demand" curve based on derived demand), and a separate "effective demand" curve, which summarizes the amount of medical care demanded at particular market prices. Because most medical care is not purchased from providers directly, but is rather obtained at subsidized prices due to insurance, the out-of-pocket prices faced by consumers are typically much lower than the market price.

The consumer sets MB=MC out of pocket, and so the "effective demand" will have a separate relationship between price and quantity than will the "marginal benefit curve" or real demand relationship. This distinction is often described under the rubric of "ex-post moral hazard" (which is again distinct from ex-ante moral hazard, which is found in any type of market with insurance).

Economic Evaluation in the United Kingdom

A large focus of health economics, particularly in the UK, is the microeconomic evaluation of individual treatments. In the UK, the National Institute for Health and Clinical Excellence (NICE) appraises certain new and existing pharmaceuticals and devices using economic evaluation.

Economic evaluation is the comparison of two or more alternative courses of action in terms of both their costs and consequences (Drummond et al.). Economists usually distinguish several types of economic evaluation, differing in how consequences are measured:

- Cost-minimization analysis
- Cost benefit analysis
- Cost-effectiveness analysis
- Cost-utility analysis

In cost minimization analysis (CMA), the effectiveness of the comparators in question must be proven to be equivalent. The 'cost-effective' comparator is simply the one which costs less (as it achieves the same outcome). In cost-benefit analysis (CBA), costs and benefits are both valued in cash terms. Cost effectiveness analysis (CEA) measures outcomes in 'natural units', such as mmHg, symptom free days, life years gained.

Finally, cost-utility analysis (CUA) measures outcomes in a composite metric of both length and quality of life, the Quality-adjusted life year (QALY). (Note there is some international variation in the precise definitions of each type of analysis).

A final approach which is sometimes classed an economic evaluation is a cost of illness study. This is not a true economic evaluation as it does not compare the costs and outcomes of alternative courses of action. Instead, it attempts to measure all the costs associated with a particular disease or condition.

These will include direct costs (where money actually changes hands, e.g. health service use, patient co-payments and out of pocket expenses), indirect costs (the value of lost productivity from time off work due to illness), and intangible costs (the 'disvalue' to an individual of pain and suffering). (Note specific definitions in health economics may vary slightly from other branches of economics.)

The five health markets typically analyzed are:

- Health care financing market
- Physician and nurses services market
- Institutional services market
- Input factors market
- Professional education market

Although assumptions of textbook models of economic markets apply reasonably well to health care markets, there are important deviations. Many states have created risk pools in which relatively healthy enrollees subsidise the care of the rest. Insurers must cope with adverse selection which occurs when they are unable to fully predict the medical expenses of enrollees; adverse selection can destroy the risk pool. Features of insurance market risk pools, such as group purchases, preferential selection ("cherry-picking"), and preexisting condition exclusions are meant to cope with adverse selection.

Insured patients are naturally less concerned about health care costs than they would if they paid the full price of care. The resulting moral hazard drives up costs, as shown by the famous RAND Health Insurance Experiment. Insurers use several techniques to limit the costs of moral hazard, including imposing copayments on patients and limiting physician incentives to provide costly care. Insurers often compete by their choice of service offerings, cost sharing requirements, and limitations on physicians.

Consumers in health care markets often suffer from a lack of adequate information about what services they need to buy and which providers offer the best value proposition. Health economists have documented a problem with supplier induced demand, whereby providers base treatment recommendations on economic, rather than medical criteria. Researchers have also documented substantial "practice variations", whereby the treatment aols on service availability to rein in inducement and practice variations.

The U.S. health care market has relied extensively on competition to control costs and improve quality. Critics question whether problems with adverse selection, moral hazard, information asymmetries, demand inducement, and practice variations can be addressed by private markets. Competition has fostered reductions in prices, but consolidation by providers and, to a lesser extent, insurers, has tempered this effect.

Though the market for health care in the U.S. is primarily coordinated by competition, there is an abundance of regulations that inhibit market efficiency. A classic example is medical licenses. Some economists argue that requiring doctors to have a medical license constrains inputs, inhibits innovation, and increases cost to consumers while largely only benefiting the doctors themselves.

Competitive Equilibrium in the Five Health Markets

While the nature of health care as a private good is preserved in the last three markets, market failures occur in the financing and delivery markets due to two reasons: (1) Perfect information about price products is not a viable assumption (2) Various barriers of entry exist in the financing markets (i.e. monopoly formations in the insurance industry)

Ideological bias in the debate about the financing and delivery health markets

The health care debate in public policy is often informed by ideology and not sound economic theory. Often, politicians subscribe to a moral order system or belief about the role of governments in public life that guides biases towards provision of health care as well. The ideological spectrum spans: individual savings accounts and catastrophic coverage, tax credit or voucher programs combined with group purchasing arrangements, and expansions of public-sector health insurance. These approaches are advocated by health care conservatives, moderates and liberals, respectively.

Other Issues

Often used synonymously with Health Economics, Medical economics, according to Culyer, is the branch of economics concerned with the application of economic theory to phenomena and problems associated typically with the second and third health market outlined above.

Typically, however, it pertains to cost-benefit analysis of pharmaceutical products and cost-effectiveness of various medical treatments. Medical economics often uses mathematical models to synthesise data from biostatistics and epidemiology for support of medical decision making, both for individuals and for wider health policy.

Peter Orszag has suggested that behavioral economics is an important factor for improving the health care system, but that relatively little progress has been made when compared to retirement policy.

6

PRICE OF TRAVEL

Before considering the calculation of the economic impacts of tourism it is worth remembering the following factors. Firstly, tourism demand fluctuates in accordance with the business cycle of the area from which tourists come. For example, international tourism grew very rapidly during the 1970s, but registered no growth at all during the recessionary years 1981-1983.

Secondly, the perceived attractiveness of a destination will vary in line with tourists' perceptions of, for example, its safety. In China, after a decade of rapid growth, international tourism receipts fell from US$2.22 billion in 1988 to US$1.80 billion in 1989 as a result of political disturbances (Tisdell and Wen, 1991). Similarly, in India, tourism levels fell during 1990-1991 due to violence and political unrest. And in Jordan, thriving tourism to archaeological sites fell away rapidly following armed confrontation in the Middle East during 1990-1991. (Combining these two factors, it can be said that tourism is subject to economic laws - yet with an element of unpredictability, the demand for tourism shifting spasmodically due to exogenous factors such as political uncertainty, wars, and currency restrictions (Diamond, 1977).)

A third source of instability is fashion. Destinations can suddenly become extremely popular. For example, tourism to certain sites in Kenya was stimulated by the film Out of

Africa (EIU International Tourism Report, 1991, Healy, 1992b). But in a relatively short time, tourists can lose interest in an area and seek alternatives elsewhere.

MEASURING ECONOMIC IMPACTS

Thousands of studies have attempted to quantify the economic impacts of tourism in various parts of the world. The vast majority measure impacts by using expenditure multipliers. The cumulative value of local economic activity is measured as revenue that has originated from tourism expenditure and that has been spent and re-spent in the local economy. A key element in multiplier calculation, therefore, is estimating the amount of expenditure that has leaked out of the local economy in the form of imports, taxes or repatriated profits. According to the World Bank, as much as 55% of the developing world's tourism profit "leaks back" to the developed world as a result of the need to import goods and services (Lindberg, 1991).

Economic studies of tourism should address each of these elements in detail, and not merely calculate expenditure multipliers. Accordingly, data on the skill-level of employment created, seasonality of employment (for example, calculating hotel employees per bed space in high and low season), direct and indirect government revenues from tourism, and ownership (foreign or domestic) of hotels, is crucial.

Particularly useful is the attempt to distinguish between the different characteristics of the various types of tourism and tourism facility. For example, for the island of Antigua, in the Caribbean, a study divided hotels into size categories, and calculated expenditure leakage (the percentage of tourist expenditure that contributed to the purchase of imported goods and services or that was repatriated as profit) for each of them (Seward and Spinrad, 1982). The study found that leakage was greater for the bigger hotels (64.8%) than for the smaller ones (38.4%). Another comparison, performed for several islands in the Caribbean, compared cruise ship tourism and "stay-over" tourism (involving at least one overnight stay). The expenditure patterns - and therefore their impacts on the economy - were likewise found to differ greatly.

Meijer (1989) conducted a similar analysis for Bolivia, but comparing organized group tourism with unorganized "rucksack tourism". He found that although the rucksack tourists spent far less on a daily basis, they stayed longer and were more likely to use small-scale, locally-owned facilities. He concluded that "rucksack tourists are at least of equal importance for La Paz as the organized tourists" and that for Bolivia as a whole "the economic impact of non-organized tourists is more than three times that of organized tourists." This type of comparative analysis could be very useful in exploring whether the economic benefits of nature-based tourism, which typically involves small-scale facilities, are greater than those of resort-based tourism. It would also help determine whether the various types of tourism are complementary or competitive, in the sense of competing for the same natural or human resources (Healy, 1992b).

Clearly then, available economic data that purport to measure the impacts of tourism give only a very limited idea of the role of tourism in the development process. Analysis of tourism's contribution to development actually requires:

- analysis of the backward and forward linkages between tourism and other sectors
- understanding of the spatial location of tourism activity
- identification of the beneficiaries of its economic and other impacts (Healy, 1992b).

Linkages

Developmental impacts of any given industry or activity depend on the nature of its interactions with suppliers (backward linkages) and its customers (forward linkages). These linkages are the basis for the calculation of multipliers.

As far as linkages are concerned, tourism may seem rather unpromising. Whether an export commodity or, in the case of domestic tourism, a final consumer good, tourism does not form a part of other activities.1 Indeed, one might say that tourism's strongest forward linkage is with itself - in relatively lightly-visited areas, tourism tends to beget more tourism, since tourists describe their experiences to others and since media accounts and guidebooks will begin to appear as an area or site gains in popularity.

Regarding backward linkages, tourism requires food, construction industry outputs, electricity and transportation. In the case of very small countries, island economies, and the least developed countries, many of these inputs must be imported. For example, for 1983, in St. Lucia, the percentage of foodstuffs of foreign origin that were consumed in hotels was: meats 86%, seafood 19%, dairy (excluding eggs) 99%, staples 30%, vegetables 35%, fruits 7%, and "other" 97% (World Bank, 1985, cited by Healy, 1992b).

Opportunities for backward linkages are greater in larger economies since they are themselves able to meet a greater percentage of the requirements for construction materials, vehicles, specialized foods, and so on. McKee (1988, cited by Healy, 1992b) observes that "in larger Third World nations...jobs will be created in industries supplying hotel and resort furnishing; athletic equipment of various sorts, including a variety of boats and deep-sea gear; and domestically produced food, not to mention resort wear and artifacts." Thus the developmental impacts of tourism may be greater in larger economies (and even if tourism constitutes a relatively small percentage of GNP, as in the case of China, India, Brazil) than in small economies for which its relative economic importance appears to be considerable (as in the case of Mauritius and the Bahamas). Moreover, many of the larger developing countries have a substantial urban middle class that is generating increasing levels of domestic tourism.

But although the size of the domestic economy sets substantial constraints on tourism's linkage effects, it appears that many opportunities to enhance linkages have been missed. For example, the existence of resort areas offers possibilities for domestic production of non-traditional foodstuffs, including fruits, vegetables and aquaculture products, but frequently, the full potential is not tapped. Innovative types of sporting goods, clothing, and souvenir items could also often be developed and even become export commodities in their own right. However, resort areas are unlikely to have advantages in manufacturing per se; they are more likely to find advantage in constant innovation of articles bought by tourists, and in promotion and marketing of them (Healy, 1992b).

Locations

Since tourism is normally spatially concentrated (i.e. tourists go where the attractions are), at least some of the economic impacts of tourism will also be concentrated, and especially if the area in question has few other economic alternatives. Indeed, nature-oriented tourists are often drawn to those very areas whose natural features - for example, mountains, harsh climates, and swamps - render agriculture and forestry difficult or not especially profitable. The Swiss Alps are a case in point. In the mid-19th Century, the overall decrease in the earnings of the farming and pastoralist economy, combined with a decreasing population in the higher regions, had pushed the area's economy into sharp decline. But all this changed with the advent of mass tourism, which most unexpectedly brought the mountain to Mohammed (Bernard, 1978, cited by Healy, 1992b).

The Alpine experience has been repeated in declining rural communities in such areas as West Virginia and the Rocky Mountains in the USA, in the Pyrenees of Spain and

France, and in the Eifel region of Germany. In each of these areas, tourism has provided a means of reducing population outflows and creating new economic growth. More negatively, however, tourism concentration in remote locations can result in "enclave tourism", in which the types of facilities and their physical location fail to take into account the needs and wishes of the surrounding community. Alternatively, the goods and services available are beyond the financial means of that community (Jenkins, 1982, cited by Healy, 1992b). In these cases, any foreign currency generated may have only a minimal effect upon the economy of the host nation. In enclave tourism, backward linkages are very weak, especially if the enclaves are controlled by multinational interests (McKee, 1988, cited by Healy, 1992b).

However, enclave tourism is sometimes adopted as a deliberate policy by a host country, in order to limit tourism's cultural or environmental impacts. In the Maldives, the government was faced with a potential cultural clash between the conservative dictates of Islam and the hedonism of "sun, sea, sand, and sex" tourism. The response was to "quarantine" tourism by building self-contained resorts on isolated, often formerly uninhabited islands (Richter, 1989, cited by Healy, 1992b). In such a situation, cultural purity is retained at the expense of backward and forward developmental linkages.

Beneficiaries

One of tourism's critical but seldom quantified impacts concerns the distribution of the benefits and costs within a given area. One means of assessing distribution is by measuring income levels within the community. It is important to determine whether the majority of tourism revenue becomes profit for a few individuals or families, or whether it is dispersed widely as payment for locally purchased goods or in the form of wages. In many communities, local power relations may dictate who benefits from opportunities arising from tourism. For example, well-connected persons may monopolize the opportunities for guiding or transporting visitors.

Even if tourism benefits are fairly widely distributed, they may not coincide with the costs. For example, protected areas may exclude hunting and foraging and swidden cultivation by local people. And although some individuals in the community may prosper by providing food, lodging and guiding services for visitors, they are not necessarily those who bear the cost of exclusion (Healy, 1992b).

A final distributional consideration is how tourism revenues interact with other economic opportunities within the family unit and the community. For some, even modest tourism revenues may be important. Bryan (1991, cited by Healy, 1992b), describes how economically-stressed ranches in the American West are now taking in guests. He notes that their hospitality operations may net as little as US$1,000 annually and seldom top US$25,000, but that nevertheless "these funds are what makes the difference for the ranch. Without this money, many family operations are sold to agribusiness, often with negative consequences for the environment." In other settings, tourism may have to be integrated with such pursuits as agriculture, forestry, grazing, or fishing. However, although tourism can be complementary to other activities, it can also be competitive.

Another aspect, sometimes controversial, is the participation of various non-national groups in the tourism business. Research in Latin America found that many small enterprises engaged in nature tourism were owned and operated by expatriates (Healy, 1988). Generally, they were resident corporate owners, and in many cases had built up their business with very little initial capital. And a close look at employment in tourism reveals that foreign nationals hold most of the management-level jobs. Jobs held by locals are usually only seasonal. Moreover, many employees migrate from other employment sectors such as agriculture, which can lead to an increased demand for agricultural imports.

Costs to stay in the World's most famous Luxury Hotels

Have you ever wondered how much it would cost to stay in all those luxurious hotels that are always on the news and in travel shows? We have too, so we decided to investigate. Below are 11 of the world's most famous 5-star hotels, along with the cost of the cheapest room available online, and the most expensive.

In at least a few cases, these hotels reserve their biggest and best suites for direct reservations, or maybe they don't want to risk having a $25,000 per night room booked as a prank by some kid with their parent's credit card. Either way, even the ones that are available are out of the price range for most of us.

Best-value Cities in Europe for Budget Travelers

We recently released our European Backpackers Index for 2011, which ranked 40 European cities by price, comparing the same set of basic budget-travel expenses in each one. While it may be interesting to see which are the cheapest and most expensive cities in the continent, choosing where to go involves more information.

Needless to say, just because a city is cheap doesn't mean you should go there, and just because it's expensive doesn't mean you should avoid it. With that in mind we've rated the region by value with this list of 11 cities where the prices of things are most worth it.

The Cheapest Country in the World is India

We've recently been compiling our Backpacker Index list for 2011, which reveals that most of the cheapest cities in Asia are alse the cheapest cities in the world. In fact, Hanoi, Vietnam comes out the least expensive of all tourist cities in the world, with the state of Goa in India coming in right behind.

Looking at the Asian cities list you'll notice that there are many destinations in Vietnam, Laos, Cambodia, and even Thailand that are extremely cheap, with the enormous metropolises of Delhi and Mumbai being significantly more expensive. The complication is that outside of India's huge cities, prices tend to go way down, so when taking the country as a whole, India is definitely the cheapest destination in the world.

World Cities by Price

If you've ever wondered which popular tourist cities around the world are cheap once you get there and which are expensive, the list below should help a lot. In 2011 Price of Travel has introduced our Backpacker Index, comparing the same exact set of expenses in over 100 worldwide cities, all translated into US dollars for ease of comparison.

This is the summary of a series of articles which went into great detail about each region on its own, and if you are considering a trip to a certain part of the world it's probably a good idea to look at the regional page for further information.

North American Cities by Price

Completing our trip around the world comparing travel costs, here's the North American Backpacker Index for 2011, which contains some surprising results. We'll next put them all together so it will be easy to see which cities and regions are truly bargains and which are better left to the rich.

The interesting thing about North America, and particularly the United States, is the pricing of hostels seems to have as much to do with how many there are in a city as it does with real estate prices. During the peak summer travel period New York City does tend to be the most expensive place to find a hostel bed, but during the rest of the year there are bargains to be found, for example.

Africa and Middle East Cities by Price

Most of Africa and much of the Middle East is mostly off-limits to many travelers, largely due to the lack of tourist infrastructure of any kind. The 9 cities listed below are among the notable exceptions, but even in some of these there are very few hostels and backpacker-friendly bars and restaurants.

Carrying on with our series that has highlighted European cities by price, Asian cities by price, South and Central American cities by price, and Australia and New Zealand cities by price, we'll now put things into just a bit more expensive by comparing them to Africa and the Middle East.

Australia & New Zealand Cities by Price

As of early 2011 Price of Travel covers over 110 cities around the world, making it easy for travelers to figure out a budget as well as normal weather for every major tourist city on the planet. Here we continue with our Backpacker Index for 2011 series, highlighting Australia and New Zealand.

Admittedly, with only four total cities in this region right now, the coverage is spotty, but fortunately these examples should provide a good range for each country as prices are generally consistent in the main tourist areas. The most dramatic factor to consider lately is the exchange rate, which, as you'll see below, has made Australia nearly as expensive as Scandinavia at the moment.

South & Central American Cities by Price

Continuing on with our series of comparing travel costs for major destinations around the world, we look at Latin America. In previous installments we checked European cities by price and Asian cities by price, so now we arrive in an area that is often ignored by much of the traveling public.

These destinations are primarily cultural stops rather than resort areas, and so far we have very limited information for the Caribbean area, but soon we'll be adding more of that and also expanding into resort destinations as well. Generally speaking, all of the cities on this list could be considered cheap, and the top group are among the cheapest travel destinations in the world, rivaling Southeast Asia and India.

7

WHAT ABOUT INSURANCE?

Health insurance, like other forms of insurance, is a form of collectivism by means of which people collectively pool their risk, in this case the risk of incurring medical expenses. The collective is usually publicly owned or else is organized on a non-profit basis for the members of the pool, though in some countries health insurance pools may also be managed by for-profit companies.

It is sometimes used more broadly to include insurance covering disability or long-term nursing or custodial care needs. It may be provided universally through government as a feature of social solidarity, as is typical in many industrial countries, or as form of government charity such as the United States Medicaid program.

It may be purchased privately on a group basis (e.g., by a firm to cover its employees) or purchased by an individual for himself or his family. In each case, the covered groups or individuals pay a fee, premium, or tax, to help protect themselves from health care expenses.

By estimating the overall risk of health care expenses, a routine finance structure (such as a monthly premium or payroll tax) can be developed, ensuring that money is available to pay for the health care benefits specified in the insurance agreement. The benefit is administered by a central organization such as a government agency, private business, or not-for-profit entity.

The concept of health insurance was proposed in 1694 by Hugh the Elder Chamberlen from the Peter Chamberlen family. In the late 19th century, "accident insurance" began to be available, which operated much like modern disability insurance. This payment model continued until the start of the 20th century in some jurisdictions (like California), where all laws regulating health insurance actually referred to disability insurance.

Accident insurance was first offered in the United States by the Franklin Health Assurance Company of Massachusetts. This firm, founded in 1850, offered insurance against injuries arising from railroad and steamboat accidents. Sixty organizations were offering accident insurance in the U.S. by 1866, but the industry consolidated rapidly soon thereafter. While there were earlier experiments, the origins of sickness coverage in the U.S. effectively date from 1890. The first employer-sponsored group disability policy was issued in 1911.

Before the development of medical expense insurance, patients were expected to pay health care costs out of their own pockets, under what is known as the fee-for-service business model. During the middle to late 20th century, traditional disability insurance evolved into modern health insurance programs. Today, most comprehensive private health insurance programs cover the cost of routine, preventive, and emergency health care procedures, and most prescription drugs, but this is not always the case.

Hospital and medical expense policies were introduced during the first half of the 20th century. During the 1920s, individual hospitals began offering services to individuals on a pre-paid basis, eventually leading to the development of Blue Cross organizations. The predecessors of today's Health Maintenance Organizations (HMOs) originated beginning in 1929, through the 1930s and on during World War II.

HOW IT WORKS

A health insurance policy is a contract between an insurance company and an individual or his sponsor (e.g. an employer). The contract can be renewable annually, monthly or be lifelong. The type and amount of health care costs that will be covered by the health insurance company are specified in advance, in a member contract or "Evidence of Coverage" booklet. The individual insured person's obligations may take several forms:

- Premium: The amount the policy-holder or his sponsor (e.g. an employer) pays to the health plan to purchase health coverage.
- Deductible: The amount that the insured must pay out-of-pocket before the health insurer pays its share. For example, policy-holders might have to pay a $500 deductible per year, before any of their health care is covered by the health insurer. It may take several doctor's visits or prescription refills before the insured person reaches the deductible and the insurance company starts to pay for care.
- Co-payment: The amount that the insured person must pay out of pocket before the health insurer pays for a particular visit or service. For example, an insured person might pay a $45 co-payment for a doctor's visit, or to obtain a prescription. A co-payment must be paid each time a particular service is obtained.
- Coinsurance: Instead of, or in addition to, paying a fixed amount up front (a co-payment), the co-insurance is a percentage of the total cost that insured person may also pay. For example, the member might have to pay 20% of the cost of a surgery over and above a co-payment, while the insurance company pays the other 80%. If there is an upper limit on coinsurance, the policy-holder could end up owing very little, or a great deal, depending on the actual costs of the services they obtain.

- Exclusions: Not all services are covered. The insured are generally expected to pay the full cost of non-covered services out of their own pockets.
- Coverage limits: Some health insurance policies only pay for health care up to a certain dollar amount. The insured person may be expected to pay any charges in excess of the health plan's maximum payment for a specific service. In addition, some insurance company schemes have annual or lifetime coverage maximums. In these cases, the health plan will stop payment when they reach the benefit maximum, and the policy-holder must pay all remaining costs.
- Out-of-pocket maximums: Similar to coverage limits, except that in this case, the insured person's payment obligation ends when they reach the out-of-pocket maximum, and health insurance pays all further covered costs. Out-of-pocket maximums can be limited to a specific benefit category (such as prescription drugs) or can apply to all coverage provided during a specific benefit year.
- Capitation: An amount paid by an insurer to a health care provider, for which the provider agrees to treat all members of the insurer.
- In-Network Provider: (U.S. term) A health care provider on a list of providers preselected by the insurer. The insurer will offer discounted coinsurance or co-payments, or additional benefits, to a plan member to see an in-network provider. Generally, providers in network are providers who have a contract with the insurer to accept rates further discounted from the "usual and customary" charges the insurer pays to out-of-network providers.
- Prior Authorization: A certification or authorization that an insurer provides prior to medical service occurring. Obtaining an authorization means that the insurer is obligated to pay for the service, assuming it matches

what was authorized. Many smaller, routine services do not require authorization.

- Explanation of Benefits: A document that may be sent by an insurer to a patient explaining what was covered for a medical service, and how payment amount and patient responsibility amount were determined.

Prescription drug plans are a form of insurance offered through some employer benefit plans in the U.S., where the patient pays a copayment and the prescription drug insurance part or all of the balance for drugs covered in the formulary of the plan. Such plans are routinely part of national health insurance programs.

Some, if not most, health care providers in the United States will agree to bill the insurance company if patients are willing to sign an agreement that they will be responsible for the amount that the insurance company doesn't pay. The insurance company pays out of network providers according to "reasonable and customary" charges, which may be less than the provider's usual fee. The provider may also have a separate contract with the insurer to accept what amounts to a discounted rate or capitation to the provider's standard charges. It generally costs the patient less to use an in-network provider.

Health Plan vs. Health Insurance (United States)

In the United States, historically, HMOs tended to use the term "health plan", while commercial insurance companies used the term "health insurance". A health plan can also refer to a subscription-based medical care arrangement offered through HMOs, preferred provider organizations, or point of service plans. These plans are similar to pre-paid dental, pre-paid legal, and pre-paid vision plans.

Pre-paid health plans typically pay for a fixed number of services (for instance, $300 in preventive care, a certain number of days of hospice care or care in a skilled nursing facility, a fixed number of home health visits, a fixed number of spinal manipulation charges, etc.). The services offered are usually at the discretion of a utilization review nurse who is often contracted through the managed care entity providing the subscription health plan. This determination may be made either prior to or after hospital admission (concurrent utilization review).

Comprehensive vs. Scheduled

Comprehensive health insurance pays a percentage of the cost of hospital and physician charges after a deductible (usually applies to hospital charges) or a co-pay (usually applies to physician charges, but may apply to some hospital services) is met by the insured. These plans are generally expensive because of the high potential benefit payout - $1,000,000 to 5,000,000 is common - and because of the vast array of covered benefits.

Scheduled health insurance plans are not meant to replace a traditional comprehensive health insurance plans and are more of a basic policy providing access to day-to-day health care such as going to the doctor or getting a prescription drug. In recent years in the USA, these plans have taken the name mini-med plans or association plans. The term "association" is often used to describe them because they require membership in an association that must exist for some other purpose than to sell insurance. Examples include the Health Care Credit Union Association.

These plans may provide benefits for hospitalization and surgical, but these benefits will be limited. Scheduled plans are not meant to be effective for catastrophic events. These plans cost much less than comprehensive health insurance. They generally pay limited benefits amounts directly to the service provider, and payments are based upon the plan's "schedule of benefits". Annual benefits maximums for a typical scheduled health insurance plan may range from $1,000 to $25,000.

Other Factors Affecting Insurance Prices

A recent study by PricewaterhouseCoopers examining the drivers of rising health care costs in the U.S. pointed to increased utilization created by increased consumer demand, new treatments, and more intensive diagnostic testing, as the most significant. People in developed countries are living longer. The population of those countries is aging, and a larger group of senior citizens requires more intensive medical care than a young, healthier population.

Advances in medicine and medical technology can also increase the cost of medical treatment. Lifestyle-related factors can increase utilization and therefore insurance prices, such as: increases in obesity caused by insufficient exercise and unhealthy food choices; excessive alcohol use, smoking, and use of street drugs. Other factors noted by the PWC study included the movement to broader-access plans, higher-priced technologies, and cost-shifting from Medicaid and the uninsured to private payers.

Other researchers note that doctors and other healthcare providers (HCPs) are rewarded for merely treating patients rather than curing them and that patients insured through employer group policies have incentives to go to the absolute best HCPs rather than the most cost-effective ones.

Comparison

The Commonwealth Fund, in its annual survey, "Mirror, Mirror on the Wall", compares the performance of the health care systems in Australia, New Zealand, the United Kingdom, Germany, Canada and the U.S. Its 2007 study found that, although the U.S. system is the most expensive, it consistently under-performs compared to the other countries. One difference between the U.S. and the other countries in the study is that the U.S. is the only country without universal health insurance coverage.

is administered by government. In France a similar system of compulsory contributions is made, but the collection is administered by non-profit organisations set up for the purpose. This is known in the United States as single-payer health care. The provision of services may be either through health care providers that may be publicly or privately owned.

An alternative funding approach is where countries implement national health insurance by legislation requiring compulsory contributions to competing insurance funds. These funds (which may be run by public bodies, private for-profit companies, or private non-profit companies), must provide a minimum standard of coverage and are not allowed to discriminate between patients by charging different rates according to age, occupation, or previous health status. To protect the interest of both patients and insurance companies, the government establishes an equalization pool to spread risks between the various funds. The government may also contribute to the equalization pool as a form of health care subsidy. This is the model used in the Netherlands.

Other countries are largely funded by contributions by employers and employees to sickness funds. With these programs, funds do not come from the government, and neither from direct private payments. This system operates in countries such as Germany and Belgium. Usually characterization is a matter of degree: systems are mixes of these three sources of funds (private, employer-employee contributions, and national/sub-national taxes). These funds are usually not for profit institutions run solely for the benefit of their members.

In addition to direct medical costs, some national insurance plans also provide compensation for loss of work due to ill-health, or may be part of wider social insurance plans covering things such as pensions, unemployment, occupational retraining, and financial support for students. National schemes have the advantage that the pool or pools tend to be very very large and reflective of the national population.

Health care costs, which tend to be high at certain stages in life such as during pregnancy and childbirth and especially in the last few years of life can be paid into the pool over a lifetime and be higher when earnings capacity is greatest to meet costs incurred at times when earnings capacity is low or non existent.

This differs from the private insurance schemes that operate in some countries which tend to price insurance year on year according to health risks such as age, family history, previous illnesses, and height/weight ratios. Thus some people tend to have to pay more for their health insurance when they are sick and/or are least able to afford it. These factors are not taken into consideration in NHI schemes. In private schemes in competitive insurance markets, these activities by insurance companies tend to act against the basic principles of insurance which is group solidarity.

Publicly Funded Health Care

Publicly funded health care is a form of health care financing designed to meet the cost of all or most health care needs from a publicly managed fund. Usually this is under some form of democratic accountability, the right of access to which are set down in rules applying to the whole population contributing to the fund or receiving benefits from it. The fund may be a not-for-profit trust which pays out for health care according to common rules established by the members or by some other democratic form. In some countries the fund is controlled directly by the government or by an agency of the government for the benefit of the entire population. This distinguishes it from other forms of private medical insurance, the rights of access to which are subject to contractual obligations between an insurer (or his sponsor) and an insurance company which seeks to make a profit by managing the flow of funds between funders and providers of health care services.

Publicly funded health care systems are usually financed in one of two ways: through taxation or via compulsory national health insurance. In compulsory insurance models, healthcare is financed from some combination of employees' salary deductions, employers' contributions, and possibly additional state funds. Insurance may cover other benefits as well as health.

When taxation is the primary means of financing health care, and sometimes with compulsory insurance, all eligible people receive the same level of cover regardless of their financial circumstances or risk factors.

Increasing Costs

As medical science advances more treatments, many increasingly expensive, become available, which increases health costs both for public and private systems. Advances in medicine, amongst other factors, increase life expectancy, leading to population aging; the proportion of the population who are working and pay tax or compulsory insurance, rather than retired, decreases at the same time as healthcare per capita becomes more expensive to provide.

VARIETIES OF PUBLIC SYSTEMS

Most developed countries, with the exception of the United States, have partially or fully publicly-funded health systems. For example, the United Kingdom has a National Health Service (NHS). Other examples would be the Medicare systems in Canada and in Australia. In Europe, a system of social insurance based on the principle of social solidarity covers eligible people from bearing the direct burden of most health care expenditure, funded by taxation during their working life.

Among countries with significant public funding of health care there are many different approaches to the funding and provision of medical services. Systems may be funded from general government revenues (as in Canada), or through a government social security system (as in France, Belgium, Japan and Germany) with a separate budget and hypothecated taxes or contributions. The proportion of the cost of care covered also differs: in Canada, all hospital care is paid for by the government, while in Japan patients must pay 10 to 30% of the cost of a hospital stay. Services provided by public systems vary. For example, the Belgian government pays the bulk of the fees for dental and eye care, while the Australian government covers eye, but not dental, care.

Publicly funded medicine may be administered and provided by the government, as in the United Kingdom as of 2011; in some systems, though, medicine is publicly funded but most hospital providers are private entities, as in Canada. The organization providing public health insurance is not necessarily a public administration, and its budget may be isolated from the main state budget. Some systems do not provide universal healthcare, or restrict coverage to public health facilities. Some countries, such as Germany, have multiple public insurance organizations linked by a common legal framework. Some, such as Holland, allow private for-profit insurers to participate.

Two-tier Health Care

Almost every major country that has a publicly funded health care system also has a parallel private system for patients who hold private medical insurance or themselves pay for treatment. In these states those able to pay have access to treatment and comforts that may not be available to those dependent upon the state system.

From the inception of the NHS model (1948), public hospitals in the United Kingdom have included "amenity beds" which would typically be siderooms fitted more comfortably, and private wards in some hospitals where for a fee more amenities are provided. Patients using these beds are in an NHS hospital for surgical treatment, and operations are generally carried out in the same operating theatres as NHS work and by the same personnel but the hospital and the physician will receive funding from an insurance company or the patient. These amenity beds do not exist in all publicly funded systems, such as in Spain. From time to time the NHS pays for private hospitals (arranged hospitals) to take on surgical cases under contract.

Policy Discussion

Many countries are seeking the right balance of public and private insurance, public subsidies, and out-of-pocket payments.Many OECD countries have implemented reforms to achieve policy goals of ensuring access to health-care, improving the quality of health care and health outcomes, allocating an appropriate level of public sector other resources to health care, whilst at the same time ensuring that services are provided in a cost-efficient and cost-effective manner (microeconomic efficiency).

A range of measures, such as better payment methods, have improved the microeconomic incentives facing providers. However, introducing improved incentives through a more competitive environment among providers and insurers has proved difficult.

In the US people die because they do not have private health insurance, or their insurance does not cover treatments they need. A 2009 Harvard study published in the American Journal of Public Health found more than 44,800 excess deaths annually in the United States due to Americans lacking health insurance, equivalent to one excess death every 12 minutes. More broadly, the total number of people in the United States, whether insured or uninsured, who die because of lack of medical care was estimated in a 1997 analysis to be nearly 100,000 per year.

8

FINANCING OPTIONS

In USA, health insurance at different levels is the best financing options. Health insurance is frequently used in the United States to describe any program that helps pay for medical expenses, whether through privately purchased insurance, social insurance or a non-insurance social welfare program funded by the government. Synonyms for this usage include "health coverage," "health care coverage" and "health benefits."

In a more technical sense, the term health insurance is used to describe any form of insurance that provides protection against the costs of medical services. This usage includes private insurance and social insurance programs such as Medicare, but excludes social welfare programs such as Medicaid. In addition to medical expense insurance, it also includes insurance covering disability or long-term nursing or custodial care needs.

The US health care system relies heavily on private and not-for-profit health insurance, which is the primary sourcc of coverage for most Americans. According to the United States Census Bureau, approximately 85% of Americans have health insurance; nearly 60% obtain it through an employer, while about 9% purchase it directly. Various government agencies provide coverage to about 28% of Americans (there is some overlap in these figures).

In 2007, there were nearly 46 million people in the US (over 15% of the population) who were without health insurance for at least part of that year. Over 1 million workers lost their health care coverage in January, February and March 2009. Approximately, 268,400 more workers lost health care coverage in March 2009 than in March 2008. Proving that today, that number is markedly higher as many workers who have lost their jobs have also lost their employer-provided health insurance.

The percentage of the non-elderly population who are uninsured has been generally increasing since the year 2000. There is considerable debate in the US on the causes of and possible remedies for this level of uninsurance as well as the impact it has on the overall US health care system.

ACCIDENT INSURANCE

This was first offered in the United States by the Franklin Health Assurance Company of Massachusetts. This firm, founded in 1850, offered insurance against injuries arising from railroad and steamboat accidents. Sixty organizations were offering accident insurance in the US by 1866, but the industry consolidated rapidly soon thereafter. While there were earlier experiments, the origins of sickness coverage in the US effectively date from 1890. The first employer-sponsored group disability policy was issued in 1911, but this plan's primary purpose was replacing wages lost due to an inability to work, not medical expenses.

Before the development of medical expense insurance, patients were expected to pay all other health care costs out of their own pockets, under what is known as the fee-for-service business model. During the middle to late 20th century, traditional disability insurance evolved into modern health insurance programs. Today, most comprehensive private health insurance programs cover the cost of routine, preventive, and emergency health care procedures, and also most prescription drugs, but this was not always the case.

Hospital and medical expense policies were introduced during the first half of the 20th century. During the 1920s, individual hospitals began offering services to individuals on a pre-paid basis, eventually leading to the development of Blue Cross organizations in the 1930s. The first employer-sponsored hospitalization plan was created by teachers in Dallas, Texas in 1929. Because the plan only covered members' expenses at a single hospital, it is also the forerunner of today's health maintenance organizations (HMOs).

Employer-sponsored health insurance plans dramatically expanded as a result of wage controls during World War II. The labor market was tight because of the increased demand for goods and decreased supply of workers during the war. Federally imposed wage and price controls prohibited manufacturers and other employers raising wages high enough to attract sufficient workers. When the War Labor Board declared that fringe benefits, such as sick leave and health insurance, did not count as wages for the purpose of wage controls, employers responded with significantly increased benefits.

Employer-sponsored health insurance was considered taxable income until 1954.

In 1965, President Lyndon B. Johnson signs the Medicare and Medicaid legislation into effect. Since their inception, the greatest challenge to the programs has been "spiraling healthcare costs, stemming largely from innovations in medical technology and pharmaceuticals." Now, as baby boomers advance toward senior citizenry, concerns about the financial sustainability of the programs frame any discussion about Medicare and Medicaid.

The debate for a public health care system in the United States has gone on for about 70 years. President Harry S.

Truman was the first United States president to propose a system of public health insurance in his November 19, 1945 address. This fund would be open to all Americans, but it would remain optional. Participants would pay monthly fees into the plan, which would cover the cost of any and all medical expenses that arose in a time of need.

The government would pay for the cost of services rendered by any doctor who chose to join the program. In addition, the insurance plan would give a cash balance to the policy holder to replace wages lost due to illness or injury. This program was denounced as a socialist approach to medicine by the American Medical Association (AMA) and did not pass.

PUBLIC HEALTH CARE COVERAGE

Public programs provide the primary source of coverage for most seniors and for low-income children and families who meet certain eligibility requirements. The primary public programs are Medicare, a federal social insurance program for seniors (generally persons aged 65 and over) and certain disabled individuals; Medicaid, funded jointly by the federal government and states but administered at the state level, which covers certain very low income children and their families; and SCHIP, also a federal-state partnership that serves certain children and families who do not qualify for Medicaid but who cannot afford private coverage. Other public programs include military health benefits provided through TRICARE and the Veterans Health Administration and benefits provided through the Indian Health Service. Some states have additional programs for low-income individuals.

Health care costs have risen more rapidly than the general economic growth and continue to do so, with the consequence that Medicare and Medicaid constitute an increasing economic burden in federal spending.

MEDICARE

In the United States, Medicare is a federal social insurance program that provides health insurance to elderly workers and their dependents, individuals who become totally and permanently disabled, and end stage renal disease (ESRD) patients. Some health care economists (Uwe Reinhardt of Princeton and Stuart Butler among others) assert that the third-party payment feature of this program has had the unintended consequence of distorting the price of medical procedures.

As a result, the Health Care Financing Administration has set up a list of procedures and corresponding prices under the Resource-Based Relative Value Scale. Recent research has found that the health trends of previously uninsured adults, especially those with chronic health problems, improves once they enter the Medicare program.

Medicare Advantage

Medicare Advantage plans expand the health care options for Medicare beneficiaries. The option for Medicare Advantage plans is a result of the Balanced Budget Act of 1997, with the intent to better control the rapid growth in Medicare spending, as well as to provide Medicare beneficiaries more choices.

Medicare Part D (Prescription Drugs)

Medicare Part D provides a private insurance option to allow Medicare beneficiaries to purchase subsidized coverage for the costs of prescription drugs. It was enacted as part of the Medicare Prescription Drug, Improvement, and Modernization Act of 2003 (MMA) and went into effect on January 1, 2006.

Medicaid

Medicaid was instituted for the very poor in 1965. Despite its establishment, the percentage of US residents who lack any form of health insurance has increased since 1994.

It has been reported that the number of physicians accepting Medicaid has decreased in recent years due to lower reimbursement rates. Medicaid is a social welfare or social protection program rather than a social insurance program.

State Children's Health Insurance Program

The State Children's Health Insurance Program (SCHIP) is a joint state/federal program to provide health insurance to children in families who earn too much money to qualify for Medicaid, yet cannot afford to buy private insurance. The statutory authority for SCHIP is under title XXI of the Social Security Act.

SCHIP programs are run by the individual states according to requirements set by the federal Centers for Medicare and Medicaid Services, and may be structured as independent programs separate from Medicaid (separate child health programs), as expansions of their Medicaid programs (SCHIP Medicaid expansion programs), or combine these approaches (SCHIP combination programs). States receive enhanced federal funds for their SCHIP programs at a rate above the regular Medicaid match.

Military Health Benefits

Health benefits are provided to active duty service members, retired service members and their dependents by the Department of Defense Military Health System (MHS). The MHS consists of a direct care network of Military Treatment Facilities and a purchased care network known as TRICARE. Additionally, veterans may also be eligible for benefits through the Veterans Health Administration.

Indian Health Service

The Indian Health Service (IHS) provides medical assistance to eligible American Indians at IHS facilities, and helps pay the cost of some services provided by non-IHS health care providers.

State Risk Pools

In 1976, some states began providing guaranteed-issuance risk pools, which enable individuals who are medically uninsurable through private health insurance to purchase a state-sponsored health insurance plan, usually at higher cost. Minnesota was the first to offer such a plan; 34 states (Alabama, Alaska, Arkansas, California, Colorado, Connecticut, Florida, Illinois, Indiana, Iowa, Kansas, Kentucky, Louisiana, Maryland, Minnesota, Mississippi, Missouri, Montana, Nebraska, New Hampshire, New Mexico, North Carolina, North Dakota, Oklahoma, Oregon, South Carolina, South Dakota, Tennessee, Texas, Utah, Washington, West Virginia, Wisconsin, Wyoming) now offer them. Plans vary greatly from state to state, both in their costs and benefits to consumers and in their methods of funding and operations. They serve a very small portion of the uninsurable market-about 182,000 people in the U.S. as of 2004, and about 200,000 in 2008.

These risk pools allow people with pre-existing conditions such as cancer, diabetes, heart disease or other chronic illnesses to be able to switch jobs or seek self-employment without fear of being without health care benefits. However, the plans are expensive, with premiums that can be double the average policy, and the pools currently cover only 1 in 25 of the so-called "uninsurable" population.

Additionally, even plans which are not expensive can leave those enrolled with little real health insurance beyond "catastrophic" insurance; for example, one insurance plan through Minnesota's high-risk pool, while costing only $215 per quarter, includes a $10,000 deductible with no preventative or other health care covered unless and until the enrollee has spent $10,000 of their own money during the year on health care.

Very sick people can accumulate large medical bills

during mandatory waiting periods before their medical expenses are covered, and there are often lifetime expenditure caps (maximums), after which the risk pool no longer pays for any medical expenses.

Efforts to pass a national pool have been unsuccessful, but some federal tax money has been awarded to states to innovate and improve their plans. With the Patient Protection and Affordable Care Act, effective by 2014, it will be easier for people with pre-existing conditions to afford regular insurance, since all insurers will be fully prohibited from discriminating against or charging higher rates for any individuals based on pre-existing medical conditions.

Pre-Existing Condition Insurance Plan

Pre-Existing Condition Insurance Plan, or PCIP, is a transitional program created in the Patient Protection and Affordable Care Act (PPACA). Those eligible for PCIP are citizens of the United States or those legally residing in the U.S., who have been uninsured for the last 6 months and "have a pre-existing condition or have been denied health coverage because of their health condition."

However, if you currently have health insurance or are enrolled in a state high risk pool, you are not eligible for PCIP, even if that coverage does not cover your medical condition. PCIP is run by the individual states or through the U.S. Department of Health and Human Services, which has a contract with the Government Employees Health Association, or GEHA, to administer benefits. Both will be funded by the federal government and provide three plan options.

These options are the standard, extended, and the Health Savings Account option. PCIP only covers the individual enrollee and does not include family members or dependents. In 2014, the Affordable Care Act provision banning discrimination based on pre-existing conditions will be implemented and PCIP enrollees will be transition into new state-based health care exchanges.

Private Health Care Coverage

Private health insurance may be purchased on a group basis (e.g., by a firm to cover its employees) or purchased by individual consumers. Most Americans with private health insurance receive it through an employer-sponsored program. According to the United States Census Bureau, some 60% of Americans are covered through an employer, while about 9% purchase health insurance directly.

The US has a joint federal/state system for regulating insurance, with the federal government ceding primary responsibility to the states under the McCarran-Ferguson Act. States regulate the content of health insurance policies and often require coverage of specific types of medical services or health care providers. State mandates generally do not apply to the health plans offered by large employers, due to the preemption clause of the Employee Retirement Income Security Act.

Employer-sponsored

Employer-sponsored health insurance is paid for by businesses on behalf of their employees as part of an employee benefit package. Most private (non-government) health coverage in the US is employment-based. Nearly all large employers in America offer group health insurance to their employees. The typical large-employer PPO plan is typically more generous than either Medicare or the Federal Employees Health Benefits Program Standard Option.

The employer typically makes a substantial contribution towards the cost of coverage. Typically, employers pay about 85% of the insurance premium for their employees, and about 75% of the premium for their employees' dependents. The employee pays the remaining fraction of the premium, usually with pre-tax/tax-exempt earnings. These percentages have been stable since 1999. Health benefits provided by employers are also tax-favored: Employee contributions can be made on a pre-tax basis if the employer offers the benefits through a section 125 cafeteria plan.

Although workers are effectively paid less than they would be, because of the cost of insurance premiums to the employer, employer-sponsored health insurance offers several benefits to workers, including economies of scale, a reduction in adverse selection pressures on the insurance pool (premiums are lower when all employees participate rather than just the sickest), and reduced income taxes. The disadvantages include disruptions related to changing jobs, the unfair regressive tax effect (high-income workers benefit far more from the tax exemption for premiums than low-income workers), and possibly increased spending on healthcare.

Costs for employer-paid health insurance are rising rapidly: since 2001, premiums for family coverage have increased 78%, while wages have risen 19% and inflation has risen 17%, according to a 2007 study by the Kaiser Family Foundation. Employer costs have risen noticeably per hour worked, and vary significantly. In particular, average employer costs for health benefits vary by firm size and occupation.

The cost per hour of health benefits is generally higher for workers in higher-wage occupations, but represent a smaller percentage of payroll. The percentage of total compensation devoted to health benefits has been rising since the 1960s. Average premiums, including both the employer and employee portions, were $4,704 for single coverage and $12,680 for family coverage in 2008.

However, in a 2007 analysis, the Employee Benefit Research Institute concluded that the availability of employment-based health benefits for active workers in the US is stable. The "take-up rate," or percentage of eligible workers participating in employer-sponsored plans, has fallen somewhat, but not sharply. EBRI interviewed employers for the study, and found that others might follow if a major employer discontinued health benefits.

Effective by January 1, 2014, the Patient Protection and Affordable Care Act will impose a $2000 per employee tax penalty on employers with over 50 employees who do not offer health insurance to their full-time workers. (In 2008, over 95% of employers with at least 50 employees offered health insurance. On the other hand, public policy changes could also result in a reduction in employer support for employment-based health benefits. Although much more likely to offer retiree health benefits than small firms, the percentage of large firms offering these benefits fell from 66% in 1988 to 34% in 2002.

Small Employer Group Coverage

According to a 2007 study, about 59% of employers at small firms (3-199 workers) in the US provide employee health insurance. The percentage of small firms offering coverage has been dropping steadily since 1999. The study notes that cost remains the main reason cited by small firms who do not offer health benefits. Small firms that are new are less likely to offer coverage than ones that have been in existence for a number of years. For example, using 2005 data for firms with fewer than 10 employees, 43% of those that had been in existence at least 20 years offered coverage, but only 24% of those that had been in existence less than 5 years did. The volatility of offer rates from year to year also appears to be higher for newer small businesses.

The types of coverage available to small employers are similar to those offered by large firms, but small businesses do not have the same options for financing their benefit plans. In particular, self-funded health care (whereby an employer provides health or disability benefits to employees with its own funds rather than contracting an insurance company) is not a practical option for most small employers.

A RAND Corporation study published in April 2008 found that the cost of health care coverage places a greater burden on small firms, as a percentage of payroll, than on larger firms. A study published by the American Enterprise Institute in August 2008 examined the effect of state benefit mandates on self-employed individuals, and found that "the larger the number of mandates in a state, the lower the probability that a self-employed person will be a significant employment generator." Beneficiary cost sharing is, on average, higher among small firms than large firms.

When small group plans are medically underwritten, employees are asked to provide health information about themselves and their covered family members when they apply for coverage. When determining rates, insurance companies use the medical information on these applications. Sometimes they will request additional information from an applicant's physician or ask the applicants for clarification.

States regulate small group premium rates, typically by placing limits on the premium variation allowable between groups (rate bands). Insurers price to recover their costs over their entire book of small group business while abiding by state rating rules. Over time, the effect of initial underwriting "wears off" as the cost of a group regresses towards the mean. Recent claim experience - whether better or worse than average - is a strong predictor of future costs in the near term. But the average health status of a particular small employer group tends to regress over time towards that of an average group. The process used to price small group coverage changes when a state enacts small group reform laws.

Insurance brokers play a significant role in helping small employers find health insurance, particularly in more competitive markets. Average small group commissions range from 2 percent to 8 percent of premiums. Brokers provide services beyond insurance sales, such as assisting with employee enrollment and helping to resolve benefits issues.

College-sponsored Health Insurance for Students

Many colleges, universities, graduate schools, professional schools and trade schools offer a school-sponsored health insurance plan. Many schools require that you enroll in the school-sponsored plan unless you are able to show that you have comparable coverage from another source.

Effective group health plan years beginning after September 23, 2010, if an employer-sponsored health plan allows employees' children to enroll in coverage, then the health plan must allow employees' adult children to enroll as well as long as the adult child is not yet age 26. Some group health insurance plans may also require that the adult child not be eligible for other group health insurance coverage, but only before 2014.

This extension of coverage will help cover one in three young adults, according to White House documents.

Federal Employees Health Benefit Plan (FEHBP)

In addition to such public plans as Medicare and Medicaid, the federal government also sponsors a health benefit plan for federal employees-the Federal Employees Health Benefits Program (FEHBP). FEHBP provides health benefits to full-time civilian employees. Active-duty service members, retired service members and their dependents are covered through the Department of Defense Military Health System (MHS). FEHBP is managed by the federal Office of Personnel Management.

"Portability" of Group Coverage

Two federal laws address the ability of individuals with employment-based health insurance coverage to maintain coverage.

The Consolidated Omnibus Budget Reconciliation Act of 1985 (COBRA) enables certain individuals with employer-sponsored coverage to extend their coverage if certain "qualifying events" would otherwise cause them to lose it. Employers may require COBRA-qualified individuals to pay the full cost of coverage, and coverage cannot be extended indefinitely. COBRA only applies to firms with 20 or more employees, although some states also have "mini-COBRA" laws that apply to small employers.

The Health Insurance Portability and Accountability Act of 1996 (HIPAA) provides for forms of both "group-to-group" and "group-to-individual" portability. When an individual moves from one employer's benefit plan to another's, the new plan must count coverage under the old plan against any waiting period for pre-existing conditions, as long as there is not a break in coverage of more than 63 days between the two plans. When certain qualified individuals lose group coverage altogether, they must be guaranteed access to some form of individual coverage. To qualify, they must have at least 18 months of prior continuous coverage. The details of access and the price of coverage are determined on a state-by-state basis.

Association Group Health Insurance

Regular health insurance is sometimes available to members of associations. Associations such as the American Bar Association and IEEE offer health insurance to their members, using an established insurance company to write the policies for a group plan.

Individually Purchased

According to the US Census Bureau, about 9% of Americans are covered under health insurance purchased directly. The range of products available is similar to those provided through employers. However, average out-of-pocket spending is higher in the individual market, with higher deductibles, co-payments and other cost-sharing provisions. Major medical is the most commonly purchased form of individual health insurance.

In the individual market, the consumer pays the entire premium without benefit of an employer contribution. While self-employed individuals receive a tax deduction for their health insurance and can buy health insurance with additional tax benefits, most consumers in the individual market do not receive any tax benefit.

Premiums vary significantly by age. In states that allow individual medical plan underwriting, premiums also vary by health status. However, with the Patient Protection and Affordable Care Act, effective by 2014, all insurers will be fully prohibited from discriminating against or charging higher rates for any individuals based on pre-existing medical conditions.

In August 2008, the Hartford Courant reported that competition was increasing in the individual health insurance market, with more insurers entering the market, an increased variety of products, and a broader spread of prices.

Individual health insurance is primarily regulated at the state level, consistent with the McCarran-Ferguson Act. Model acts and regulations promulgated by the National Association of Insurance Commissioners (NAIC) provide some degree of uniformity state to state. These models do not have the force of law and have no effect unless they are adopted by a state. They are, however, used as guides by most states, and some states adopt them with little or no change.

Types of Medical Insurance

Traditional Indemnity or Fee-for-service

Early hospital and medical plans offered by insurance companies paid either a fixed amount for specific diseases or medical procedures (schedule benefits) or a percentage of the provider's fee. The relationship between the patient and the medical provider was not changed. The patient received medical care and was responsible for paying the provider. If the service was covered by the policy, the insurance company was responsible for reimbursing or indemnifying the patient based on the provisions of the insurance contract ("reimbursement benefits"). Health insurance plans that are not based on a network of contracted providers, or that base payments on a percentage of provider charges, are still described as indemnity or fee-for-service plans.

Blue Cross & Blue Shield Plans

The Blue Cross and Blue Shield Association (BCBSA) is a federation of 39 separate health insurance organizations and companies in the United States. Combined, they directly or indirectly provide health insurance to over 100 million Americans. BCBSA insurance companies are franchisees, independent of the association (and traditionally each other), offering insurance plans within defined regions under one or both of the association's brands. Blue Cross Blue Shield insurers offer some form of health insurance coverage in every U.S. state. They also act as administrators of Medicare in many states or regions of the U.S., and provide coverage to state government employees as well as to the federal government employees under a nationwide option of the Federal Employees Health Benefit Plan.

Health Maintenance Organizations

A health maintenance organization (HMO) is a type of managed care organization (MCO) that provides a form of health care coverage that is fulfilled through hospitals, doctors, and other providers with which the HMO has a contract. The Health Maintenance Organization Act of 1973 required employers with 25 or more employees to offer federally certified HMO options.

Unlike traditional indemnity insurance, an HMO covers only care rendered by those doctors and other professionals who have agreed to treat patients in accordance with the HMO's guidelines and restrictions in exchange for a steady stream of customers. Benefits are provided through a network of providers. Providers may be employees of the HMO ("staff model"), employees of a provider group that has contracted with the HMO ("group model"), or members of an independent practice association ("IPA model"). HMOs may also use a combination of these approaches ("network model").

Managed Care

The term managed care is used to describe a variety of techniques intended to reduce the cost of health benefits and improve the quality of care. It is also used to describe organizations that use these techniques ("managed care organization"). Many of these techniques were pioneered by HMOs, but they are now used in a wide variety of private health insurance programs. Through the 1990s, managed care grew from about 25% US employees with employer-sponsored coverage to the vast majority.

Rise of Managed Care in the US

Year	Conventional plans	HMOs	PPOs plans	POS	HDHP /SOs
1998	14%	27%	35%	24%	~
1999	10%	28%	39%	24%	~
2000	8%	29%	42%	21%	~
2001	7%	24%	46%	23%	~
2002	4%	27%	52%	18%	~

2003	5%	24%	54%	17%	~
2004	5%	25%	55%	15%	~
2005	3%	21%	61%	15%	~
2006	3%	20%	60%	13%	4%
2007	3%	21%	57%	15%	5%
2008	2%	20%	58%	12%	8%

Network-based Managed Care

Many managed care programs are based on a panel or network of contracted health care providers. Such programs typically include:

- A set of selected providers that furnish a comprehensive array of health care services to enrollees;
- Explicit standards for selecting providers;
- Formal utilization review and quality improvement programs;
- An emphasis on preventive care; and
- Financial incentives to encourage enrollees to use care efficiently.

Provider networks can be used to reduce costs by negotiating favorable fees from providers, selecting cost effective providers, and creating financial incentives for providers to practice more efficiently. A survey issued in 2009 by America's Health Insurance Plans found that patients going to out-of-network providers are sometimes charged extremely high fees.

Network-based plans may be either closed or open. With a closed network, enrollees' expenses are generally only covered when they go to network providers. Only limited services are covered outside the network-typically only emergency and out-of-area care. Most traditional HMOs were closed network plans. Open network plans provide some coverage when an enrollee uses non-network provider, generally at a lower benefit level to encourage the use of network providers. Most preferred provider organization plans are open-network (those that are not are often described as exclusive provider organizations, or EPOs), as are point of service (POS) plans.

The terms "open panel" and "closed panel" are sometimes used to describe which health care providers in a community have the opportunity to participate in a plan. In a "closed panel" HMO, the network providers are either HMO employees (staff model) or members of large group practices with which the HMO has a contract. In an "open panel" plan the HMO or PPO contracts with independent practitioners, opening participation in the network to any provider in the community that meets the plan's credential requirements and is willing to accept the terms of the plan's contract.

Other Managed Care Techniques

Other managed care techniques include such elements as disease management, case management, wellness incentives, patient education, utilization management and utilization review. These techniques can be applied to both network-based benefit programs and benefit programs that are not based on a provider network. The use of managed care techniques without a provider network is sometimes described as "managed indemnity."

Blurring Lines

Over time, the operations of many Blue Cross and Blue Shield operations have become more similar to those of commercial health insurance companies. However, some Blue Cross and Blue Shield plans continue to serve as insurers of last resort. Similarly, the benefits offered by Blues plans, commercial insurers, and HMOs are converging in many respects due to market pressures. One example is the convergence of preferred provider organization (PPO) plans offered by Blues and commercial insurers and the point of service plans offered by HMOs.

Historically, commercial insurers, Blue Cross and Blue Shield plans, and HMOs might be subject to different regulatory oversight in a state (e.g., the Department of Insurance for insurance companies, versus the Department of Health for HMOs). Today, it is common for commercial insurance companies to have HMOs as subsidiaries, and for HMOs to have insurers as subsidiaries (the state license for an HMO is typically different from that for an insurance company). At one time the distinctions between traditional indemnity insurance, HMOs and PPOs were very clear; today, it can be difficult to distinguish between the products offered by the various types of organization operating in the market.

The blurring of distinctions between the different types of health care coverage can be seen in the history of the industry's trade associations. The two primary HMO trade associations were the Group Health Association of America and the American Managed Care and Review Association. After merging, they were known as American Association of Health Plans (AAHP). The primary trade association for commercial health insurers was the Health Insurance Association of America (HIAA). These two have now merged, and are known as America's Health Insurance Plans (AHIP).

New Types of Medical Plans

One approach to addressing increasing premiums, dubbed "consumer driven health care," received a boost in 2003, when President George W. Bush signed into law the Medicare Prescription Drug, Improvement, and Modernization Act. The law created tax-deductible Health Savings Accounts (HSAs), untaxed private bank accounts for medical expenses, which can be established by those who already have health insurance. Withdrawals from HSAs are only penalized if the money is spent on non-medical items or services.

Funds can be used to pay for qualified expenses, including doctor's fees, Medicare Parts A and B, and drugs, without being taxed. Consumers wishing to deposit pre-tax funds in an HSA must be enrolled in a high-deductible insurance plan with a number of restrictions on benefit design; in 2007, qualifying plans must have a minimum deductible of US$1,050. HSAs enable healthier individuals to pay less for insurance and bank money for their own future health care expenses.

HSAs are one form of tax-preferenced health care spending accounts. Others include Flexible Spending Accounts (FSAs), Archer Medical Savings Accounts (MSAs), which have been superseded by the new HSAs (although existing MSAs are grandfathered), and Health Reimbursement Accounts (HRAs). These accounts are most commonly used as part of an employee health benefit package. While there are currently no government-imposed limits to FSAs, legislation currently being reconciled between the House of Representatives and Senate would impose a cap of $2,500. While both the House and Senate bills would adjust the cap to inflation, approximately 7 million Americans who use their FSAs to cover out-of-pocket health care expenses greater than $2,500 would be forced to pay higher taxes and health care costs.

In July 2009, Save Flexible Spending Plans, a national grassroots advocacy organization, was formed to protect against the restricted use of FSAs in health care reform efforts, Save Flexible Spending Accounts is sponsored by the Employers Council on Flexible Compensation (ECFC), a non-profit organization "dedicated to the maintenance and expansion of the private employee benefits on a tax-advantaged basis". ECFC members include companies such as WageWorks Inc., a benefits provider based in San Mateo, California.

Most FSA participants are middle income Americans, earning approximately $55,000 annually. Individuals and families with chronic illnesses typically receive the most benefit from FSAs; even when insured, they incur annual out-of-pocket expenses averaging $4,398 . Approximately 44 percent of Americans have one or more chronic conditions.

Because Limited Medical Benefit Plans pay for routine care and do not pay for catastrophic care, they do not provide equivalent financial security to a major medical plan. Annual benefit limits can be as low as $2,000. Lifetime maximums can be very low as well.

One option that is becoming more popular is the discount medical card. These cards are not insurance policies, but provide access to discounts from participating health care providers. While some offer a degree of value, there are serious potential drawbacks for the consumer.

Health Insurance Market Concentration

The US health insurance market is highly concentrated, as leading insurers have carried out over 400 mergers from the mid-1990s to the mid-2000s. In 2000, the two largest health insurers (Aetna and UnitedHealth Group) had total membership of 32 million. By 2006 the top two insurers, WellPoint and UnitedHealth, had total membership of 67 million. The two companies together had more than 36% of the national market for commercial health insurance. The AMA has said that it "has long been concerned about the impact of consolidated markets on patient care."

A 2007 AMA study found that in 299 of the 313 markets surveyed, one health plan accounted for at least 30% of the combined health maintenance organization (HMO)/ preferred provider organization (PPO) market. The US Department of Justice has recognised this percentage of market control as conferring substantial monopsony power in the relations between insurer and physicians.

Other Types of Health Insurance (non-medical)

While the term "health insurance" is most commonly used by the public to describe coverage for medical expenses, the insurance industry uses the term more broadly to include other related forms of coverage, such as disability income and long-term care insurance.

Disability Income Insurance

Disability income (DI) insurance pays benefits to individuals who lose their ability to work due to injury or illness. DI insurance replaces income lost while the policyholder is unable to work during a period of disability (in contrast to medical expense insurance, which pays for the cost of medical care). For most working age adults, the risk of disability is greater than the risk of premature death, and the resulting reduction in lifetime earnings can be significant. Private disability insurance is sold on both a group and an individual basis. Policies may be designed to cover long-term disabilities (LTD coverage) or short-term disabilities (STD coverage). Business owners can also purchase disability overhead insurance to cover the overhead expenses of their business while they are unable to work.

A basic level of disability income protection is provided through the Social Security Disability Insurance (SSDI) program for qualified workers who are totally and permanently disabled (the worker is incapable of engaging in any "substantial gainful work" and the disability is expected to last at least 12 months or result in death).

Long-term Care Insurance

Long-term care (LTC) insurance reimburses the policyholder for the cost of long-term or custodial care services designed to minimize or compensate for the loss of functioning due to age, disability or chronic illness. LTC has many surface similarities to long-term disability insurance. There are at least two fundamental differences, however. LTC policies cover the cost of certain types of chronic care, while long-term-disability policies replace income lost while the policyholder is unable to work. For LTC, the event triggering benefits is the need for chronic care, while the triggering event for disability insurance is the inability to work.

Private LTC insurance is growing in popularity in the US. Premiums have remained relatively stable in recent years. However, the coverage is quite expensive, especially when consumers wait until retirement age to purchase it. The average age of new purchasers was 61 in 2005, and has been dropping.

Supplemental Coverage

Private insurers offer a variety of supplemental coverages in both the group and individual markets. These are not designed to provide the primary source of medical or disability protection for an individual, but can assist with unexpected expenses and provide additional peace of mind for insureds. Supplemental coverages include Medicare supplement insurance, hospital indemnity insurance, dental insurance, vision insurance, accidental death and dismemberment insurance and specified disease insurance.

Supplemental coverages are intended to:

- Supplement a primary medical expense plan by paying for expenses that are excluded or subject to the primary plan's cost-sharing requirements (e.g., co-payments, deductibles, etc.);
- Cover related expenses such as dental or vision care;
- Assist with additional expenses that may be associated with a serious illness or injury.

Medicare Supplement policies are designed to cover expenses not covered (or only partially covered) by the "original Medicare" (Parts A & B) fee-for-service benefits. They are only available to individuals enrolled in Medicare Parts A & B. Medigap plans may be purchased on a guaranteed issue basis (no health questions asked) during a six-month open enrollment period when an individual first becomes eligible for Medicare. The benefits offered by Medigap plans are standardized.

Hospital Indemnity Insurance

Hospital indemnity insurance provides a fixed daily, weekly or monthly benefit while the insured is confined in a hospital. The payment is not dependent on actual hospital charges, and is most commonly expressed as a flat dollar amount. Hospital indemnity benefits are paid in addition to any other benefits that may be available, and are typically used to pay out-of-pocket and non-covered expenses associated with the primary medical plan, and to help with additional expenses (e.g., child care) incurred while in the hospital.

Scheduled Health Insurance Plans

Scheduled health insurance plans are an expanded form of Hospital Indemnity plans. In recent years, these plans have taken the name mini-med plans or association plans. These plans may provide benefits for hospitalization, surgical, and physician services. However, they are not meant to replace a traditional comprehensive health insurance plan. Scheduled health insurance plans are more of a basic policy providing access to day-to-day health care such as going to the doctor or getting a prescription drug, but these benefits will be limited and are not meant to be effective for catastrophic events.

Payments are based upon the plan's "schedule of benefits" and are usually paid directly to the service provider. These plans cost much less than comprehensive health insurance. Annual benefit maximums for a typical scheduled health insurance plan may range from $1,000 to $25,000.

Dental Insurance

Dental insurance helps pay for the cost of necessary dental care. Few medical expense plans include coverage for dental expenses. About 97% of dental benefits in the United States is provided through separate policies from carriers-both stand-alone and medical affiliates-that specialize in this coverage. Discount dental programs are also available. These do not constitute insurance, but provide participants with access to discounted fees for dental work.

Vision Care Insurance

Vision care insurance provides coverage for routine eye care and is typically written to complement other medical benefits. Vision benefits are designed to encourage routine eye examinations and ensure that appropriate treatment is provided.

Specified Disease

Specified disease provides benefits for one or more specifically identified conditions. Benefits can be used to fill gaps in a primary medical plan, such as co-payments and deductibles, or to assist with additional expenses such as transportation and child care costs.

Accidental Death and Dismemberment (AD&D) insurance

AD&D insurance is offered by group insurers and provides benefits in the event of accidental death. It also provides benefits for certain specified types of bodily injuries (e.g., loss of a limb or loss of sight) when they are the direct result of an accident.

STATUS OF THE UNINSURED

Based on self-reported census data, in 2007, more than 45 million people in the US (15.3% of the population) were without health insurance as defined in the questions asked. The percentage of the non-elderly population who are uninsured has been generally increasing since the year 2000. Among the uninsured population, some 37 million were employment-age adults (ages 18 to 64), and more than 27 million worked at least part time. About 38% of the uninsured live in households with incomes over $50,000.

According to the Census Bureau, nearly 36 million of the uninsured are legal US citizens. Another 9.7 million are non-citizens, but the Census Bureau does not distinguish in its estimate between legal non-citizens and illegal immigrants. It has been estimated that nearly one fifth of the uninsured population is able to afford insurance, almost one quarter is eligible for public coverage, and the remaining 56% need financial assistance (8.9% of all Americans). An estimated 5 million of those without health insurance are considered "uninsurable" because of pre-existing conditions.

The costs of treating the uninsured must often be absorbed by providers as charity care, passed on to the insured via cost-shifting and higher health insurance premiums, or paid by taxpayers through higher taxes.

A report published by the Kaiser Family Foundation in April 2008 found that economic downturns place a significant strain on state Medicaid and SCHIP programs. The authors estimated that a 1% increase in the unemployment rate would increase Medicaid and SCHIP enrollment by 1 million, and increase the number uninsured by 1.1 million. State spending on Medicaid and SCHIP would increase by $1.4 billion (total spending on these programs would increase by $3.4 billion). This increased spending would occur at the same time state government revenues were declining. During the last downturn, the Jobs and

Growth Tax Relief Reconciliation Act of 2003 (JGTRRA) included federal assistance to states, which helped states avoid tightening their Medicaid and SCHIP eligibility rules. The authors conclude that Congress should consider similar relief for the current economic downturn.

Death

Since people who lack health insurance are unable to obtain timely medical care, they have a 40 percent higher risk of death in any given year than those with health insurance, according to a study published in the American Journal of Public Health. The study estimated that in 2005 in the United States, there were 45,000 deaths associated with lack of health insurance.

The United States' system of using health insurance as a means of financing health care costs has been criticized. The following are examples of such criticisms

- While "private plans are attractive because of their ability to be responsive to consumer demands for choice and their innovations resulting from both the profit motive and desire to attract a larger enrollment base," they also have disadvantages. Industry consolidation "has not led to strong insurers who are willing or able to negotiate effectively with dominant hospital systems," and "insurance markets have become dominated by a small number of large insurers" with "shadow pricing" by smaller insurers.
- Insurance companies have high administrative costs. Private health insurers are a significant portion of the U.S. economy directly employing (in 2004) almost 470,000 people at an average salary of $61,409.
- Health insurance companies are not actually providing traditional insurance, which involves the pooling of risk, because the vast majority of purchasers actually do face the harms that they are "insuring" against. Instead, as

Edward Beiser and Jacob Appel have separately argued, health insurers are better thought of as low-risk money managers who pocket the interest on what are really long-term healthcare savings accounts.

- According to a study by a pro-health reform group published February 11, the nation's largest five health insurance companies posted a 56 percent gain in 2009 profits over 2008. The insurers (Wellpoint, UnitedHealth, Cigna, Aetna and Humana) cover the majority of Americans with health insurance.

9

HEALTH TOURISM PROVIDER

If you choose, a trained Destination Program Manager (DPM) will accompany you to all of your medical appointments. After your procedure, we arrange for transfer to your hotel or resort for relaxation & recuperation. Your DPM will continue to be available at all times during your health tourism experience.

Before you leave the country, your physician will see you again. He or she will communicate with your local doctor, if required, and confirm that you are ready to fly home.

In an attempt to rein in exploding medical costs, a growing number of health insurance companies are offering their customers, both individuals and employers, an opportunity to get their health care overseas. Some medical and dental procedures overseas can cost up to 80 percent less, excluding travel costs, than in the states.

Medical tourism, according to the international nonprofit organization Medical Tourism Association, is a practice whereby "people who live in one country travel to another country to receive medical, dental and surgical care," which they do "because of affordability, better access to care or a higher level of quality of care." One of the principles of the Association is to provide unbiased information and education for health insurance companies, patients, and employers about available hospitals and medical and dental services.

In the past, most medical tourists were wealthy or uninsured. Today, however, more and more of them have health insurance. According to a 2008 survey conducted by Deloitte Center for Health Solutions, nearly 40 percent of Americans said they would travel overseas to receive medical treatment if the cost was cut in half and the quality of care was comparable.

As more and more Americans make the trip overseas-80,000 traveled to Bangkok's Bumrungrad International Hospital in 2006 alone, according to Managed Care magazine-health insurance providers are slowing joining in. Among them are Aetna, Blue Cross Blue Shield of South Carolina, and Georgia-based BasicPlus Insurance Services, and an increasing number of others are making inquiries.

One concern about surgeries and medical procedures performed overseas is follow-up care. Patients need to know how such care will be handled, especially if complications arise. Some US insurance providers have agreements with foreign hospitals to coordinate post-procedure care.

Some services, such as hip and knee surgery, heart valve replacements, spinal fusions, coronary artery bypass graft surgery, and many dental surgeries, are good candidates for medical tourists. Others, such as bone marrow transplants, need special follow-up care and should be done at home.

Individuals whose health insurance provider offers overseas medical care should consider several factors. Generally, people who have a high deductible plan may find medical tourism economically worthwhile, and some employers are even willing to pick up the travel expenses because the savings to them is considerable as well. High out-of-pocket expenses are common with dental coverage, which makes overseas dental care trips popular as well. Medical tourists should also take along a friend or family member to help them deal with the medical system in a foreign country.

Approximately 750,000 Americans were medical tourists in 2007 and, according to Deloitte Center for Health Solutions, about twice that number will make the trip in 2010. As the number of health insurance companies who offer this option to its premium payers grows, so will the number of individuals and employers who will pack their bags.

A recent paper presented at the Annual Meeting of the European Society of Human Reproduction and Embryology in Rome highlights the growth of "infertility tourism" at a time when many medical tourism businesses are feeling the pinch of the recession.

The article, "Cross border reproductive care in six European countries" provides a review of inbound infertility tourism to six European countries receiving patients - Belgium, Czech Republic, Denmark, Slovenia, Spain and Switzerland. Data was collected from 46 centres in these countries. Patients came from 49 different countries, but almost two thirds came form only four countries - Italy (31.8%), Germany (14.4%), The Netherlands (12.1%) and France (8.7%).

DRIVERS OF INFERTILITY TOURISM

Why are these infertile couples crossing borders for infertility treatment? It varies from country to country but the main driver is the law on infertility treatments within the home country. This is the predominant reason for patients coming from Italy, France, Germany, Norway and Sweden.

Italian law banned sperm donation in 2004; German law bans egg donation; in France, assisted conception for single women or same sex couples is illegal and there is a ban on advertising for egg donors; regulation regarding donor anonymity affect Scandinavians and British patients; some countries have regulations that limit reimbursement of assisted conception to a maximum age.; some countries have legal limits on the amount that can be paid to donors thus reducing availability of sperm and eggs.

Difficulties in accessing treatment at home were a driver for a third of UK patients, and a wish for "anonymous" donation was expressed by around one in five patients.

There's also some indication of specific cross border flows: Italians favour Switzerland and Spain, the Germans prefer Czech Republic, the Dutch and French opt for Belgium.

18.3% of patients were looking for semen donation, 22.8% for egg donation and 3.4% for embryo donation.

Market opportunity for medical tourism businesses?

The study estimated that "a minimum estimated number of 11 000-14 000 patients per year" visits the six countries in the study; it may well be much higher than this.

If you're in the medical tourism business, download the paper; it's a useful insight into the opportunities in infertility tourism and to the kind of patients that seek it..... which should be a major influence on your marketing. Understanding your market is key to the success of any medical tourism business. For example, the internet was a frequent source of information about infertility treatment abroad in Sweden (73.6%), Germany (65.0%) and the UK (58.5%).

View of Dr Neil on Medical Tourism

Dr Neil Lunt, Senior Lecturer in Public Policy in Management at the University of York gave an academic perspective on medical tourism to Caroline Ratner of IMTJ about medical tourism at the recent medical tourism workshop at the Infection 2009 conference in Birmingham.

How did you become interested in medical tourism?

I have always worked in the area of health and social services. I was living in New Zealand for a while and when I returned to the UK in 2007 I realised that the country had become more European in outlook which was a very interesting change and because of my work I began looking into the growth of patient mobility.

Why do you think there has been a steady increase in medical tourism in Europe?

I think the increase is due to the availability of low costs flights within Europe which has led to increased mobility and the notion of the possibility of increased patient flow throughout Europe has led more people to travel for surgery. The idea that NHS patients and self paying patients in the UK can travel is increasing and one of the reasons is that it is getting harder for some patients to access certain parts of the NHS, i.e. it may be their age or their location that makes access difficult to certain services.

What other social/economic factors are contributing to the growth of medical tourism

There is an increased willingness of people to travel for surgery and a large part of this is the growth and acceptability of cosmetic surgery in our culture. In the last ten years cosmetic surgery has gone from being the preserve of the rich and famous to becoming acceptable and accessible to a much wider range of people from all types of socio-economic groups. Cheap flights, the growth of celebrity culture and body obsession and the easy access to information about how to access treatment abroad has contributed enormously to these changes. As a result having cosmetic surgery, both here in the UK and overseas is now available and acceptable to large numbers of people from different demographics who previously would never have considered it.

What do you see as the downside of the growth of medical tourism?

One of the major downsides is the as yet lack of formal research; a lot of current research is anecdotal and piecemeal. There is no proper research into botched surgeries, we only hear about surgeries that have gone wrong in the press, there is no impartial research funded by trusts, the industry or other medical organisations into the actual numbers that are travelling, how many surgeries are going wrong, how people are making their choices about procedures and where to go. While there is a growing amount of information available overall, the general public are not that well informed.

What kind of research into the medical tourism market is needed?

I would be very interested in talking to people who have had a range of treatments about what motivated them to have surgery and their decision making process. I'd also like to know how they judged their experience, the quality of the surgery and treatment, the clinical outcomes, whether they needed post-operative treatment for infections etc., or whether they needed medical care on their return to their home country.

What's interesting is to me at the moment is how people make their choices; do they book directly or do they go through a facilitator? How do they conceptualise the risks of what they are doing, how do they make their choices? What's more important to patients? Price or quality and reputation? If they are using the internet for research what tools are they using to ascertain whether the information they are using to make a decision is credible? These are all important questions for the industry to consider.

What about other issues in medical tourism such as ethics and safety records?

Ethical issues are another area that needs examining. Questions need to be raised when you merge medical procedures that could be considered controversial with commercial considerations. When you get the two things together you could get certain treatments offered by commercial operators that could raise ethical questions. i.e. what is the age ceiling for IVF treatment? Likewise, some controversial treatments available abroad might not be countenanced by doctors or sanctioned here and patients need to be aware of the potential implications of having these kinds of treatments.

Safety is another area that needs to be looked into as standards vary widely throughout the world. The NHS is very upfront about its safety record and there is transparency of information. NHS patients have access to a lot of information which can't be said about some European and other destinations and the information that is available does not always bear up to public scrutiny.

In fact, worse than no safety records, or evidence, is misleading evidence. Stories have emerged from a major hospital in Thailand about statistics about the number of foreign patients that make no sense; the numbers just don't stack up. Obviously the hospital is trying to give a good impression but the information is not verifiable and this is the problem. Hospitals should be giving prospective patients information that is independently scrutinised and monitored and medical tourists need to be aware of this.

Another grey area is accreditation, what do kite marks, and accreditation show patients? What does it all mean? There needs to be industry wide clarification so that patients can confidently make choices based on unbiased information.

What responsibility do you think brokers and facilitators have towards their customers?

Questions need to be asked about what brokers/ facilitators do and what are their boundaries and responsibilities and how their role is defined. Integrity is of high importance here when brokers are advising medical tourists on where to go. How are brokers providing information? On what basis are they basing their recommendations? Are they being based on solid, impartial information or otherwise. I think it is important that the industry sets standards in this area and that those facilitators remain unaffiliated to clinics and hospitals.

Many hospitals and clinics, especially in poorer countries and the developing world claim that treating foreign patients helps the local economy and thus contributes to higher standards of care for local patients. Do you agree?

Many countries like India, Thailand and Eastern European countries claim that the influx of medical tourists helps the local community but in countries like India, which has high levels of poverty there are ethical issues that need to be considered when foreign patients are treated in local hospitals. Of course foreign patients will improve the local economy but do they medically help the locals who might need different types of treatments to the ones being sold to the medical tourists. It could be that a hospital provides very high tech treatment for foreign patients while squeezing out necessary low-tech services that locals need.

ROLE OF TRAVEL AGENCY

A travel agency is a retail business that sells travel related products and services to customers on behalf of suppliers such as airlines, car rentals, cruise lines, hotels, railways, sightseeing tours and package holidays that combine several products. In addition to dealing with ordinary tourists most travel agencies have a separate department devoted to making travel arrangements for business travelers and some travel agencies specialize in commercial and business travel only. There are also travel agencies that serve as general sales agents for foreign travel companies, allowing them to have offices in countries other than where their headquarters are located.

The British company Cox & Kings is sometimes said to be the oldest travel agency in the world, but this rests upon the services that the original bank, established in 1758, supplied to its wealthy clients. The modern travel agency first appeared in the second half of the 19th century. Thomas Cook, in addition to developing the package tour, established a chain of agencies in the last quarter of the 19th century, in association with the Midland Railway. They not only sold their own tours to the public, but in addition, represented other tour companies. Other British pioneer travel agencies were Dean and Dawson, the Polytechnic Touring Association and the Co-operative Wholesale Society. The oldest travel agency in North America is Brownell Travel; on July 4, 1887, Walter T. Brownell led ten travelers on a European tour, setting sail from New York on the SS Devonia.

Travel agencies became more commonplace with the development of commercial aviation, starting in the 1920s. Originally, travel agencies largely catered to middle and upper class customers, but the post-war boom in mass-market package holidays resulted in travel agencies on the main streets of most British towns, catering to a working class clientèle, looking for a convenient way to book overseas beach holidays.

Operations

As the name implies, a travel agency's main function is to act as an agent, that is to say, selling travel products and services on behalf of a supplier. Consequently, unlike other retail businesses, they do not keep a stock in hand. A package holiday or a ticket is not purchased from a supplier unless a customer requests that purchase. The holiday or ticket is supplied to them at a discount. The profit is therefore the difference between the advertised price which the customer pays and the discounted price at which it is supplied to the agent. This is known as the commission. A British travel agent would consider a 10-12% commission as a good arrangement. In Australia, all individuals or companies that sell tickets are required to be licensed as a travel agent.

In some countries, airlines have stopped giving commission to travel agencies. Therefore, travel agencies are now forced to charge a percentage premium or a standard flat fee, per sale. However, some companies still give them a set percentage for selling their product. Major tour companies can afford to do this, because if they were to sell a thousand trips at a cheaper rate, they still come out better than if they sell a hundred trips at a higher rate. This process benefits both parties.

Other commercial operations are undertaken, especially by the larger chains. These can include the sale of in-house insurance, travel guide books and timetables, car rentals, and the services of an on-site Bureau de change, dealing in the most popular holiday currencies.

The majority of travel agents have felt the need to protect themselves and their clients against the possibilities of commercial failure, either their own or a supplier's. They will advertise the fact that they are surety bonded, meaning in the case of a failure, the customers are guaranteed either an equivalent holiday to that which they have lost or if they prefer, a refund.

Many British and American agencies and tour operators are bonded with the International Air Transport Association (IATA), for those who issue air tickets, Air Travel Organisers' Licensing (ATOL) for those who order tickets in, the Association of British Travel Agents (ABTA) or the American Society of Travel Agents (ASTA), for those who sell package holidays on behalf of a tour company.

A travel agent is supposed to offer impartial travel advice to the customer. However, this function almost disappeared with the mass-market package holiday and some agency chains seemed to develop a 'holiday supermarket' concept, in which customers choose their holiday from brochures on racks and then book it from a counter. Again, a variety of social and economic changes have now contrived to bring this aspect to the fore once more, particularly with the advent of multiple, no-frills, low-cost airlines.

Commissions

Most travel agencies operate on a commission-basis, meaning that the compensation from the airlines, car rentals, cruise lines, hotels, railways, sightseeing tours and tour operators, etc., is expected in form of a commission from their bookings. Most often, the commission consists of a set percentage of the sale.

In the United States, most airlines pay no commission at all to travel agencies. In this case, an agency usually adds a service fee to the net price.

TYPES OF AGENCIES

There are three different types of agencies in the UK: Multiples, Miniples and Independent Agencies. The former comprises a number of national chains, often owned by international conglomerates, like Thomson Holidays, now a subsidiary of TUI AG, the German multinational. It is now quite common for the large mass-market tour companies to purchase a controlling interest in a chain of travel agencies, in order to control the distribution of their product. (This is an example of vertical integration.) The smaller chains are often based in particular regions or districts.

In the United States, there are four different types of agencies: Mega, Regional, Consortium and Independent

Agencies. American Express and the American Automobile Association (AAA) are examples of mega travel agencies.

Independent Agencies usually cater to a special or niche market, such as the needs of residents in an upmarket commuter town or suburb or a particular group interested in a similar activity, such as sporting events, like football, golf or tennis.

There are two approaches of travel agencies. One is the traditional, multi-destination, out-bound travel agency, based in the originating location of the traveler and the other is the destination focused, in-bound travel agency, that is based in the destination and delivers an expertise on that location. At present, the former is usually a larger operator like Thomas Cook, while the latter is often a smaller, independent operator.

Consolidators

Airline consolidators and other types of travel consolidators and wholesalers are high volume sales companies that specialize in selling to niche markets. They may or may not offer various types of services, at a single point of access. These can be hotel reservations, flights or car-rentals, for example. Sometimes the services are combined into vacation packages, that include transfers to the location and lodging. These companies do not usually sell directly to the public, but act as wholesalers to retail travel agencies. Commonly, the sole purpose of consolidators is to sell to ethnic niches in the travel industry. Usually, no consolidator offers everything, they may only have contracted rates to specific destinations. Today, there are no domestic consolidators, with some exceptions for business class contracts.

Travel agencies have been accused of employing a number of restrictive practices, the chief of which is known as 'racking'. This is the practice of displaying only the brochures of those travel companies whose holidays they wish to sell, the ones that pay them the most commission. Of course, the average customer tends to think that these are the only holidays on offer and is unaware of the possible alternatives.

Conversely, by limiting the number of companies that a travel agency represents, this can bring a better and more profitable, working relationship between the agency and its suppliers. Travel agencies can then obtain special benefits for their customers, from a supplier, by concentrating their bookings with that supplier. Some examples of these special benefits would be room upgrades or the waiver of change and cancellation fees.

Package Holiday

With general public access to the Internet, many airlines and other travel companies began to sell directly to passengers. As a consequence, airlines no longer needed to pay the commissions to travel agents on each ticket sold. Since 1997, travel agencies have gradually been disintermediated, by the reduction in costs caused by removing layers from the package holiday distribution network. However, travel agents remain dominant in some areas such as cruise vacations where they represent 77% of bookings and 73% of packaged travel.

In response, travel agencies have developed an internet presence of their own by creating travel websites, with detailed information and online booking capabilities. Several major online travel agencies include: Expedia, Voyages-sncf.com, Travelocity, Orbitz, CheapTickets, Priceline, CheapOair and Hotwire.com. Travel agencies also use the services of the major computer reservations systems companies, also known as Global Distribution Systems (GDS), including: SABRE, Amadeus CRS, Galileo CRS and Worldspan, which is a subsidiary of Travelport, allowing them to book and sell airline tickets, hotels, car rentals and other travel related services. Some online travel websites allow visitors to compare hotel and flight rates with multiple companies for free. They often allow visitors to sort the travel packages by amenities, price, and proximity to a city or landmark.

Travel agents have applied dynamic packaging tools to provide fully bonded (full financial protection) travel at prices equal to or lower than a member of the public can book online. As such, the agencies' financial assets are protected in addition to professional travel agency advice.

All travel sites that sell hotels online work together with GDS, suppliers and hotels directly to search for room inventory. Once the travel site sells a hotel, the site will try to get a confirmation for this hotel. Once confirmed or not, the customer is contacted with the result. This means that booking a hotel on a travel website will not necessarily result in an instant answer. Only some hotels on a travel website can be confirmed instantly (which is normally marked as such on each site). As different travel websites work with different suppliers together, each site has different hotels that it can confirm instantly. Some examples of such online travel websites that sell hotel rooms are Expedia, Orbitz and WorldHotel-Link.

The comparison sites, such as Kayak.com, TripAdvisor and SideStep search the resellers site all at once to save time searching. None of these sites actually sell hotel rooms.

Often tour operators have hotel contracts, allotments and free sell agreements which allow for the immediate confirmation of hotel rooms for vacation bookings.

Mainline service providers are those that actually produce the direct service, like various hotels chains or airlines that have a website for online bookings. Portals will serve a consolidator of various airlines and hotels on the internet. They work on a commission from these hotels and airlines. Often, they provide cheaper rates than the mainline service providers as these sites get bulk deals from the service providers. A meta search engine on the other hand, simply culls data from the internet on real time rates for various search queries and diverts traffic to the mainline service providers for an online booking. These websites usually do not have their own booking engine.

10

GUIDE TO HEALTH TOURISM

Every year thousands of people require treatment for dreaded diseases like cancer, heart diseases, kidney diseases, liver diseases, orthopedics, pediatric diseases, etc. Many people need treatment at highly specialized hospitals abroad. In this site, we have collected the names, descriptions, contact information, and website links of reputed specialized hospitals from Asia. Medical tourism is a rapidly growing phenomenon in today's world. People from developed and developing countries are seeking low cost and extremely good quality medical treatment in Asian countries and other countries of the world. Many Asian countries have set up specialized departments in their countries to encourage medical tourism in their countries. Many top hospitals in Asian countries have set up dedicated departments to cater to the international patients.

Asia has become the most popular destination for medical tourists in the world. Asia offers high quality, world-standard medical treatment at only 20 percent of the cost of treatment in the USA and the UK. The quality of treatment here is of world-class standard with many of the doctors holding western qualifications. Medical tourism is rapidly growing in Asia with the number of medical tourists to Asian countries increasing by about 20 to 30 percent each year. It is estimated that the medical tourism in Asia will be worth US$ 4 billion by the year 2012.

Medical tourism in India is growing at a rate of 30 per cent per year. It is estimated that India will earn US$2.2 billion a year through medical tourism by 2012. Singapore, which is another important center for medical tourism in Asia aims to receive one million foreign patients every year. It is estimated that medical tourism in Singapore will earn it above US$1.6 billion annually. Malaysia, which is also among the top four medical tourism centers of the world expects to earn upto US$590 million within five years. Altogether, medical tourism in Asia is expected to earn it US$4.4. billion by 2012. Currently, the number of medical tourists is estimated to be 1.32 million. These medical tourists to Asia come to seek medical treatment from all over the world. Medical tourists come from US and Europe, but it is estimated that most of the medical tourists to the medical tourism centers of Asia come from within Asia.

Should you or your close ones require higher treatment for their diseases, you will find here all the information about which will be the best hospital for you. So, browse through the hospital information given here and find out which is the hospital that is most suitable for providing the treatment that you seek.

There are 37 countries in Asia. Given here is a list of hospitals in the major countries of Asia, like Hong Kong, India, Thailand, Malaysia, Singapore, and Russia. Click on the country names to find a list of the major hospitals in these countries and also information about medical tourism in these countries. You can find detailed information about the treatment options available for diseases like cancer, heart disease, orthopedics, cosmetic surgery in these countries. Nowadays, many Asian countries offer the latest medical treatment for various diseases, on par with most western countries, but often at a fraction of the cost. Many Asian countries have become much in demand centers for medical tourism. In these websites, you will find complete information about medical tourism in these Asian countries.

American Journal of Public Health

The American Journal of Public Health is a monthly peer-reviewed medical journal published by the American Public Health Association covering health policy and public health. The journal was established in 1911 and its stated mission is "to advance public health research, policy, practice, and education." The journal occasionally publishes themed supplements. The editor-in-chief is Mary E. Northridge.

The journal contains the following departments:

- Government, Politics, and Law - public health arguments grounded in critical analysis
- Health Policy and Ethics Forum - debates on public health issues
- Field Action Reports - reports on practice-based programs and initiatives with potential to advance the public's health
- Framing Health Matters - articles featuring work in the social sciences and other disciplines
- Faces of Public Health and Going Public - profiles of outstanding leaders and examples of vital public health work
- Images of Public Health, Public Health Then and Now, and Voices From the Past - stories from public health history still relevant today
- Highlights and guidance from the world of statistics

The American Journal of Public Health was voted one of the 100 most influential journals in biology and medicine over the last 100 years by Special Libraries Association. According to the Journal Citation Reports, the 2009 impact factor is 4.241, ranking it second out of 95 titles in the category "Public, Environmental and Occupational Health" of the Social Sciences Edition and 9th out of 122 in the same category in the Science Edition.

The journal is abstracted and indexed in Ageline, Applied Social Science Index and Abstracts, Biological Abstracts, Chemical Abstracts Service, CINAHL, EMBASE/Excerpta Medica, Food Science and Technology Abstracts, MEDLINE,Psychological Abstracts, PsycINFO, Science Citation Index, Scopus, and Statistical Reference Index/Lexis Nexis.

Journal of Public Health Policy

The Journal of Public Health Policy is a peer-reviewed medical journal established in 1980 by Milton Terris. It covers the field of public health and is the official journal of the National Association for Public Health Policy..

According to the 2009 Journal Citation Reports, the journal has an impact factor of 1.326, ranking it 42nd out of 69 in the category "Health Care Sciences & Services" and 75th out of 122 in the category "Public, Environmental & Occupational Health".

The journal is abstracted and indexed in CSA Sociological Abstracts, EMBASE, Index Medicus/MEDLINE, PsycINFO, Science Citation Index Expanded, Scopus, and Social Sciences Citation Index.

Public Health

Public health is "the science and art of preventing disease, prolonging life and promoting health through the organized efforts and informed choices of society, organizations, public and private, communities and individuals" (1920, C.E.A. Winslow). It is concerned with threats to the overall health of a community based on population health analysis.

The population in question can be as small as a handful of people or as large as all the inhabitants of several continents (for instance, in the case of a pandemic). Public health is typically divided into epidemiology, biostatistics and health services. Environmental, social, behavioral, and occupational health are other important subfields.

The focus of public health intervention is to prevent rather than treat a disease through surveillance of cases and the promotion of healthy behaviors. In addition to these activities, in many cases treating a disease may be vital to preventing it in others, such as during an outbreak of an infectious disease. Hand washing, vaccination programs and distribution of condoms are examples of public health measures.

The goal of public health is to improve lives through the prevention and treatment of disease. The United Nations' World Health Organization defines health as "a state of complete physical, mental and social well-being and not merely the absence of disease or infirmity."

The focus of a public health intervention is to prevent rather than treat a disease through surveillance of cases and the promotion of healthy behaviors. In addition to these activities, in many cases treating a disease can be vital to preventing its spread to others, such as during an outbreak of infectious disease or contamination of food or water supplies. Vaccination programs and distribution of condoms are examples of public health measures.

Most countries have their own government public health agencies, sometimes known as ministries of health, to respond to domestic health issues. In the United States, the front line of public health initiatives are state and local health departments. The United States Public Health Service (PHS), led by the Surgeon General of the United States, and the Centers for Disease Control and Prevention, headquartered in Atlanta, are involved with several international health activities, in addition to their national duties.

There is a vast discrepancy in access to health care and public health initiatives between developed nations and developing nations. In the developing world, public health infrastructures are still forming. There may not be enough trained health workers or monetary resources to provide even a basic level of medical care and disease prevention. As a result, a large majority of disease and mortality in the developing world results from and contributes to extreme poverty. For example, many African governments spend less than USD$10 per person per year on health care, while, in the United States, the federal government spent approximately USD$4,500 per capita in 2000.

Many diseases are preventable through simple, non-medical methods. For example, research has shown that the simple act of hand washing can prevent many contagious diseases.

Public health plays an important role in disease prevention efforts in both the developing world and in developed countries, through local health systems and through international non-governmental organizations.

The two major postgraduate professional degrees related to this field are the Master of Public Health (MPH) or MSc in Public Health or allied fields. Doctoral studies in this field include Doctor of Public Health (DrPH) and PhD in a subspeciality of greater Public Health disciplines. DrPH is regarded as a leadership degree and PhD is more an academic degree.

HISTORY OF PUBLIC HEALTH

In some ways, public health is a modern concept, although it has roots in antiquity. From the beginnings of human civilization, it was recognized that polluted water and lack of proper waste disposal spread ,communicable diseases (theory of miasma). Early religions attempted to regulate behavior that specifically related to health, from types of food eaten, to regulating certain indulgent behaviors, such as drinking alcohol or sexual relations. The establishment of governments placed responsibility on leaders to develop public health policies and programs in order to gain some understanding of the causes of disease and thus ensure social stability prosperity, and maintain order.

The term "healthy city" used by today's public health advocates reflects this ongoing challenge to collective physical well-being that results from crowded conditions and urbanization.

Early Public Health Interventions

By Roman times, it was well understood that proper diversion of human waste was a necessary tenet of public health in urban areas. The Chinese developed the practice of variolation following a smallpox epidemic around 1000 BC. An individual without the disease could gain some measure of immunity against it by inhaling the dried crusts that formed around lesions of infected individuals. Also, children were protected by inoculating a scratch on their forearms with the pus from a lesion. This practice was not documented in the West until the early-18th century, and was used on a very limited basis. The practice of vaccination did not become prevalent until the 1820s, following the work of Edward Jenner to treat smallpox.

During the 14th century Black Death in Europe, it was believed that removing bodies of the dead would further prevent the spread of the bacterial infection. This did little to stem the plague, however, which was most likely spread by rodent-borne fleas. Burning parts of cities resulted in much greater benefit, since it destroyed the rodent infestations. The development of quarantine in the medieval period helped mitigate the effects of other infectious diseases. However, according to Michel Foucault, the plague model of governmentality was later controverted by the cholera model. A Cholera pandemic devastated Europe between 1829 and 1851, and was first fought by the use of what Foucault called "social medicine", which focused on flux, circulation of air, location of cemeteries, etc. All those concerns, born of the miasma theory of disease, were mixed with urbanistic concerns for the management of populations, which Foucault designated as the concept of "biopower". The German conceptualized this in the Polizeiwissenschaft ("Science of police").

The science of epidemiology was founded by John Snow's identification of a polluted public water well as the source of an 1854 cholera outbreak in London. Dr. Snow believed in the germ theory of disease as opposed to the prevailing miasma theory. Although miasma theory correctly teaches that disease is a result of poor sanitation, it was based upon the prevailing theory of spontaneous generation. Germ theory developed slowly: despite Anton van Leeuwenhoek's observations of Microorganisms, (which are now known to cause many of the most common infectious diseases) in the year 1680, the modern era of public health did not begin until the 1880s, with Louis Pasteur's germ theory and production of artificial vaccines.

Other public health interventions include latrinization, the building of sewers, the regular collection of garbage followed by incineration or disposal in a landfill, providing clean water and draining standing water to prevent the breeding of mosquitoes. This contribution was made by Edwin Chadwick in 1843 who published a report on the sanitation of the working class population in Great Britain at the time. So began the inception of the modern public health. The industrial revolution had initially caused the spread of disease through large conurbations around workhouses and factories. These settlements were cramped and primitive and there was no organised sanitation. Disease was inevitable and its incubation in these areas was encouraged by the poor lifestyle of the inhabitants....

MODERN PUBLIC HEALTH

As the prevalence of infectious diseases in the developed world decreased through the 20th century, public health began to put more focus on chronic diseases such as cancer and heart disease. An emphasis on physical exercise was reintroduced.

In America, public health worker Dr. Sara Josephine Baker lowered the infant mortality rate using preventative methods. She established many programs to help the poor in New York City keep their infants healthy. Dr. Baker led teams of nurses into the crowded neighborhoods of Hell's Kitchen and taught mothers how to dress, feed, and bathe their babies. After World War I many states and countries followed her example in order to lower infant mortality rates.

During the 20th century, the dramatic increase in average life span is widely credited to public health achievements, such as vaccination programs and control of infectious diseases, effective safety policies such as motor-vehicle and occupational safety, improved family planning, chlorination of drinking water, smoke-free measures, and programs designed to decrease chronic disease.

Meanwhile, the developing world remained plagued by largely preventable infectious diseases, exacerbated by malnutrition and poverty. Front-page headlines continue to present society with public health issues on a daily basis: emerging infectious diseases such as SARS, making its way from China to Canada and the United States; prescription drug benefits under public programs such as Medicare; the increase of HIV-AIDS among young heterosexual women and its spread in South Africa; the increase of childhood obesity and the concomitant increase in type II diabetes among children; the impact of adolescent pregnancy; and the ongoing social, economic and health disasters related to the 2004 Tsunami and Hurricane Katrina in 2005. These are all ongoing public health challenges.

Since the 1980s, the growing field of population health has broadened the focus of public health from individual behaviors and risk factors to population-level issues such as inequality, poverty, and education. Modern public health is often concerned with addressing determinants of health across a population, rather than advocating for individual behaviour change. There is a recognition that our health is affected by many factors including where we live, genetics, our income, our educational status and our social relationships - these are known as "social determinants of health."

A social gradient in health runs through society, with those that are poorest generally suffering the worst health. However even those in the middle classes will generally have worse health outcomes than those of a higher social stratum. The new public health seeks to address these health inequalities by advocating for population-based policies that improve health in an equitable manner.

Schools of Public Health

In the United States, the Welch-Rose Report of 1915 has been viewed as the basis for the critical movement in the history of the institutional schism between public health and medicine because it led to the establishment of schools of public health supported by the Rockefeller Foundation. The report was authored by William Welch, founding dean of the Johns Hopkins Bloomberg School of Public Health, and Wycliffe Rose of the Rockefeller Foundation. The report focused more on research than practical education.

Some have blamed the Rockefeller Foundation's 1916 decision to support the establishment of schools of public health for creating the schism between public health and medicine and legitimizing the rift between medicine's laboratory investigation of the mechanisms of disease and public health's nonclinical concern with environmental and social influences on health and wellness.

Even though schools of public health had already been established in Europe and North Africa, the US had still maintained the traditional system of housing faculties of public health within their medical institutions. However, a year following the Welch-Rose report, the Johns Hopkins School of Hygiene and Public Health was founded in 1916. By 1922, schools of public health were established in Columbia, Harvard and Yale universities. By 1999 there were twenty nine schools of public health in the US, enrolling around fifteen thousand students.

Over the years, the types of students and training provided have also changed. In the beginning, students who enrolled in public health schools had already obtained a medical degree. However, in 1978, 69% of students enrolled in public health schools had only a bachelors degree. Public health school training had evolved from a second degree for medical professionals to a primary public health degree with a focus on the six core disciplines of biostatistics, epidemiology, health services administration, health education, behavioral science and environmental health.

Education and Training

Schools of public health offer a variety of degrees which generally fall into two categories: professional or academic. Professional degrees are oriented towards practice in public health settings. The Master of Public Health (M.P.H.), Doctor of Public Health (Dr.PH.), Doctor of Health Science (D.H.Sc.) and the Master of Health Care Administration (M.H.A.) are examples of degrees which are geared towards people who want careers as practitioners of public health in health departments, managed care and community-based organizations, hospitals and consulting firms among others.

Master of Public Health (M.P.H.) degrees broadly fall into two categories, those that put more emphasis on an understanding of epidemiology and statistics as the scientific basis of public health practice and those that include a more eclectic range of methodologies.

A Master of Science of Public Health (M.S.P.H.) is similar to an M.P.H. but is considered an academic degree (as opposed to a professional degree) and places more emphasis on quantitative methods and research. The same distinction can be made between the Dr.PH. and the D.H.Sc. The Dr.PH is considered a professional degree and the D.H.Sc. is an academic degree.

Academic degrees are more oriented towards those with interests in the scientific basis of public health and preventive medicine who wish to pursue careers in research, university teaching in graduate programs, policy analysis and development, and other high-level public health positions. Examples of academic degrees are the Master of Science (M.S.), Doctor of Philosophy (Ph.D.), Doctor of Science (Sc.D.), and Doctor of Health Science (D.H.Sc.). The doctoral programs are distinct from the M.P.H. and other professional programs by the addition of advanced coursework and the nature and scope of a dissertation research project.

The Association of Schools of Public Health represents Council on Education for Public Health (CEPH) accredited schools of public health. Delta Omega is the honorary society for graduate studies in public health. The society was founded in 1924 at the Johns Hopkins School of Hygiene and Public Health. Currently, there are approximately 68 chapters throughout the United States and Puerto Rico.

IMPORTANCE OF PUBLIC HEALTH PROGRAMS

Today, most governments recognize the importance of public health programs in reducing the incidence of disease, disability, and the effects of aging, although public health generally receives significantly less government funding compared with medicine. In recent years, public health programs providing vaccinations have made incredible strides in promoting health, including the eradication of smallpox, a disease that plagued humanity for thousands of years.

An important public health issue facing the world currently is HIV/AIDS and Antibiotic resistance leading to the reemergence of diseases such as Tuberculosis.

Another major public health concern is diabetes, according to the World Health Organization, at least 171 million people worldwide suffered from diabetes. Its incidence is increasing rapidly, and it is estimated that by the year 2030, this number will double. However, in a June 2010 editorial in the medical journal The Lancet, the authors opined that "The fact that type 2 diabetes, a largely preventable disorder, has reached epidemic proportion is a public health humiliation.

A controversial aspect of public health is the control of Tobacco smoking,Smoking smoking behaviours caused by smoking have been threatening public health because it requires a long term strategy for improving unlike the communicable diseases which take a shorter period to be improved. The reason for this is because communicable diseases have been at the top as a global health priority while non communicable diseases have been at the bottom as a global health priority.

Simultaneously, global health policy making is increasingly aligned with industrial and trade policies, and is being done hand in hand with business, thus weakening the firewalls necessary for effective regulation and normative actions both at national and global. Many nations have implemented major initiatives to cut smoking, such as increased taxation and bans on smoking in some or all public places.

Proponents argue by presenting evidence that smoking is one of the major killers in all developed countries, and that therefore governments have a duty to reduce the death rate, both through limiting passive (second-hand) smoking and by providing fewer opportunities for smokers to smoke. Opponents say that this undermines individual freedom and personal responsibility and worry that the state may be emboldened to remove more and more choice in the name of better population health overall. However, proponents counter that inflicting disease on other people via passive smoking is not a human right, and in fact smokers are still free to smoke in their own homes.

There is also a link between public health and veterinary public health which deals with zoonotic diseases, diseases that can be transmitted from animals to humans. Obesity is a growing problem that public health is facing. WHO's latest projections indicate that globally in 2008 approximately 1.5 billion adults (age 20+) were overweight and of these, more than 200 million men and nearly 300 million women were obese. WHO further projects that by 2015, approximately 2.3 billion adults will be overweight and more than 700 million will be obese. Nearly 43 million children under the age of 5 years were overweight globally in 2010.

The U.S. is the leading country with 30.6% of its population being obese. Mexico follows behind with 24.2% and the United Kingdom with 23%. The weighted average percentage among 30 countries is 14.1%. Obesity is responsible for 325,000 deaths every year. It was considered a problem in high-income countries, but now it is on the rise in low-income countries, especially in urban settings. There are many Public Health programs dedicated to this issue of obesity. Many of these program's objectives is to promote a healthy diet, nutrition, and physical activity.

Applications in Healthcare

As well as seeking to improve population health through the implementation of specific population-level interventions, public health professionals, (Francesco, Sam and Ermanno are prime examples as they helped to make the 1992 survey of England and Wales) also seek to improve population health by improving the contribution of medical care to life extension and quality of life.

Such improvements could be identified by assessing what need for health services existed within the population, and:

1. Assessing current services
2. Ascertaining requirements as expressed by professionals, public and other stakeholders
3. Identifying the most appropriate interventions
4. Considering the effect on resources
5. Agreeing and implementing any necessary changes

In addition public health professionals can improve population health through:

1. Assessing evidence of effectiveness and cost-effectiveness for proposed interventions
2. The evaluation of healthcare to determine whether the activity in question is meeting its objectives
3. Supporting decision making in healthcare and planning health services

Skin Renovation Medicines

Study considered anti-aging skin care products, mainly to correct the most common question is' What skin renovation medicines have so far proven to be effective? Useful Information collected regarding anti-flood measures to repair an old market is the most effective way to implement anti-aging skin care methods that are suitable for the aging of the skin.

To retrieve the eternal beauty and to restore their youth, go with the anti get skin care supplements and more. Anti-aging cosmetic products can improve their nutritional aspect that from the inside. And it can be a pure procedure. No need to go to a painful surgery. Anti more skin care products can dramatically change the way you look better and make you feel young. Can the problem of the aging process with anti-aging skin care that life presents to dry or oily skin. You will be able to actually place during the aging of a couple of years with anti care therapies achieve more and enjoy the excitement of youthful life.

Anti-aging cosmetics anti aging generally include active components that support the pores of the skin and the ability to take pure free radicals, age spots, and chemical toxins that impede healthy skin, and improve your pores and skin suppleness and elasticity. An excellent anti old can reduce droopy skin and wrinkles. Skin Care Anti aging supplements work in Concord with full body, and balancing the supply of anti aging mandatory requirements for food and thus make your skin glow and look younger for a long time interval.

Vision And Dental Insurance

For most of us who work and receive medical benefits through an employer, once a year, we are asked to select insurance plans for health benefits. Every year we have also given the opportunity to choose additional coverage for dental insurance and vision. Some employers may not offer coverage and dental and vision coverage, but in some cases they may cover up to certain amounts or some basic services. For example, federal employees have their own federal employee's dental and vision insurance program.

Usually when we go with the group insurance from employers, we can get a discount rate of vision and dental plans. It is highly recommended to review the dental plans and vision to see what services are covered and you can make cost-benefit analysis. The comparison of the services offered to the amounts of the monthly premiums you pay.

Most times it will come out a winner, since dental and vision package can save you money in the long term. Most major suppliers that the plan is available at a reasonable price. Some of the plan is related to health insurance, but some are available independently. At the same time can also understand that your dental or vision review is long overdue, and it's time to go to the dentist or eye doctor.

Best Protein Supplement

With carbohydrates and lipids, proteins are one of three macronutrients that we need in our daily diet. Unfortunately, few people receive sufficient amounts only of their diet, so we are always looking for the best protein supplement available so we present four reasons why you should take a supplement.

1. Most diets are deficient in quality protein - vegetarians and vegans, who eat no animal protein, are particularly likely to be insufficient, but they suffer the majority of Americans to some degree of impairment. The supplements are essential in providing balance to your diet. You should also note that problems may arise as a protein in the diet of poor consumers and could re-apply for the filling.
2. After training to recover - if you participate in intensive cardio or weight training, then take a supplement cocktail session after the protein is essential to ensure adequate recovery. The liquids are digested more easily and more quickly by the body of a cocktail are recommended to allow your body to begin its rapid muscle recovery. You must have your cocktail as soon as possible after your workout.
3. Active lifestyle - your body will decompose, and therefore require more protein if you lead an active life. Running the length of time cardio activity can actually cause your body needs even more intensive weight training.

Best Muscle Gain

One of the biggest questions that people ask in the gym is what exercise is best for gaining muscle in a specific area of the body. Now there's an easy question to answer. People are different and if something works for me, so this does not mean it will automatically for you. So what's the answer?

The large compound exercises generally work well, but for beginners it is not always the case and it takes a while for newcomers to get the hang of it. So will it be? If you are a beginner or you do not know what the right approach, then you should stick with what works for you. If you fancy something works then do not change because someone else to do another exercise for that body part. As I said people are different and our body reacts to different exercises.

For example I must have a high degree of press for my chest to my work upper chest while the other guys do not; it's just how my body works. So stay close, listen to your body, most of the time your body is straight. Sometimes you hate to use the favorite. So catch your favorite exercises, but to mix them with a couple of new and some of them grow on you.

Removal Treatment Of Genital Warts

There is no cure or treatment that eliminates HPV infection, so the only current treatment is likely to remove lesions on the skin caused by a virus. However, the removal of genital warts does not substantially reduce the spread of the virus, and genital warts are common. None of the opportunities available remedy is a complete or substantially better than the other.

Signs and symptoms of genital warts in women than men are equal; the difference is that they are much more frequent. Venereal warts are found among women in the form of spots and blisters on the outside, in the genital area. Small blisters may appear in the vagina, which explains why the Pap test

(Pap test) is required for women of all ages to avoid complications that can occur if the disease is not treated properly.

Altsberglotion successfully treats genital warts. Due to the nature of the organic solvent as a necessary ingredient of balms, we do not offer the treatment of genital warts in mucous membranes (oral cavity, dental, and the male organ within the genitals). This is due to organic solvent physical wounds of the skin and many problems can occur in the form of damage, irritation, burning and itching. Therefore, treatment is recommended if the warts are in the skin around the genital area. In this case, the treatment is effective and in many cases the treatment of external genital warts is the removal of the residence.

Tips On Pain Fight Against Cancer

Cancer patients from both the mental and physical discomfort and severe pain. The pain depends on the stage of the tumor and the tolerance of the power of one. This pain also cause depression and anxiety in patients. Although cancer pain is due to the disease itself or its side effects, may be issued with medication. Here are some tips that will help them to form relieves the pain they suffer.

1. You should consult your doctor and ask him to suggest some medications or injections may provide some relief to the patient.
2. You can also search for your medical care and go to massage therapy. This massage therapy will reduce the physical demands of the patient and relieve depression and anxiety, he goes through because of pain.
3. Ayurveda, a form of alternative medicine may also help control cancer pain.
4. Yoga and relaxation exercise the mind and body of the patient. Relaxes the senses of patients, and plays a vital role in the treatment of pain. regular walking and not

only helps keep the body's metabolism, but also helps control the side effects that is caused by a disease like cancer.

5. Try and record the pain when it came time date and intensity. Also mention things that had worsening of pain and how long it lasted. This journal will help health care provider to get a clear idea about the disease and determine the treatment that can relieve the patient of pain.

Natural Beauty Care Tips

They are beautiful not only apply to the appearance rather than inner beauty. It is about having a healthy and clean. Trying to look young is, in principle, all the time, if you are a woman or even human. But we all know that aging is something natural, that we can not stop, but there are ways to slow down this process. And the best way to do this is to use natural methods that are cheap or even free. Here are some beauty tips for free.

Help purify water and cool the body, which is especially important in hot weather. Be aware of what you eat, this can be a simple trick but very difficult to do. Stay away from spicy, fatty and junk food. Eat plenty of green foods and fruits, also foods rich in fiber, vitamins and minerals that are good for the body.Sun is the only source of vitamin D in order to stay under the sun is also a good thing. But do not over do it, because of sunburn and skin cancer can occur.

Its deficiency can cause pale skin, and severe allergic reactions. Use creams, Aloe Vera helps to produce new skin cells and removes dead. Get enough rest is also very important, as it would be enough sleep, make sure you get seven hours of sleep per day to stay healthy. With this, daily exercise may also help maintain your health inside and out.

Natural Way to Lose Weight

Most of this is not a shred of scientific reasoning behind it, even worse, some may even be harmful. Their effectiveness varies between zero and a moderate, but for those who need to lose a few pounds fast, here are some safe, foolproof.

A change in diet - Studies blame the large amounts of sugar, sodium and cholesterol found in the food chain of junk food and weight gain. Why do people gain weight is easy. More than foster their ovens food high in calories but few nutrients. Cheeseburger, for example, contains the maximum amount of fat very active in the 150-pound person would have one day. But, lettuce, tomato and pickles, and does not meet the five percent or even your daily fiber and vitamin C are needed. Hamburger buns and all the others you may need to twelve percent of calories in carbohydrates.

Have a cheeseburger for lunch and dinner to give your body too much protein and fat, and deprived of its essential as vitamins and fiber. It does not help that these "meals" orders from our favorite fast food joint that are made from sugar, soft drinks, water and caffeine, once again, empty calories. They give you energy, but that's all they give you. Going on a diet does not mean getting stuck eating bland "fat" foods. Is to choose healthy alternatives. Snacks of apples or a cup of fruit instead of fries and sandwiches and fruit smoothies instead of Slurpees help you lose weight.

Back Pain Medication Tips

Try getting a massage to relieve your pain. The movement will help stimulate blood circulation, which accelerates the healing process in place. It will also relax the muscles in the region. If your pain is caused by a voltage or a pulled muscle, it may be a very effective form of pain relief. Also, try the heat treatment. The heat helps to relax the pain away. For a much deeper penetration of heat, infrared heating pad test. Healthy Back Institute offers a variety of infrared heating pads in different sizes to suit your needs and budget.

Although it can be very tempting to be there when you hurt your back, try to resist this temptation. Stagnant for too long causes stiffness and decreased blood flow. This will result in even more pain. So try to stay active. Moderate exercise such as walking can often help relieve tension and help the region recover.

If you suffer from frequent back pain, check your posture. Slouching is a major cause of back pain. If you spend much time sitting at work, trying to stay upright. Consider investing in a mattress support, such as those provided by the Healthy Back Institute. They are supported by cushions of different shapes and sizes and even a massage on your back as you feel. What better way to get rid of her back pain to receive a massage while you work?

Other Ways To Help Asthma

Asthma can be a chronic problem for most people from infancy to adulthood. Asthma is a respiratory disease caused by inflammation and narrowing of the airways of the lung. Some of its symptoms are cough, rapid breathing, wheezing and dyspnea. And these symptoms may be worsened by poor breathing techniques. When the air does not get the patient is also difficult to breathe out of the way causes the patient to an asthma attack.

If you have asthma, you can help yourself by manipulating your breathing pattern to relaxation and deep breathing exercises. This will help you control your breathing muscles and in turn contribute to an improvement in your condition. Besides breathing exercises, you can also ask for help the healing properties of nature, using alternative treatments using garlic and honey. Garlic is regarded as an effective ingredient when it comes to natural remedies asthma.

You can try it by cooking the garlic in milk. What is said to be very useful if you experience symptoms of asthma and is especially recommended for those who are in the early stages of asthma. All you have to do is boil ten cloves of garlic in half a glass of milk and drink before going to bed. Another possible solution is for you to use honey. You can get a glass of hot water and add a teaspoon of honey. Drink this mixture very slowly before going to bed.

11

HOSPITAL HINTS

Has your doctor said you need a medical test that has to be done in the hospital? Do you need surgery? Most people worry when they have to stay overnight in the hospital. Learning more about what to expect and about people who work in hospitals can help.

Visiting someone who is sick isn't always easy, but it can be an enjoyable time and it should primarily be a comfort for the patient. Many family members and friends find it difficult to visit someone who is sick. If the person is in the hospital, it may be more difficult for some to visit because of past negative experiences they have had at a hospital. Many visitors are anxious or find it stressful to be around a patient because they are dealing with their own fears of sickness. It is natural to hesitate in seeing someone you love or care about, who is in pain or seriously ill. Unfortunately, many people end up not visiting, because they do not know what to do or say to help.

Most patients I have spoken to just want the company. They want to feel loved and thought about. They do not want to be forgotten, though they might be out of the "social loop".

I know when I was sick and had visitors it was a welcome distraction from the reality of what was going on. It was nice to at least try to forget and feel "normal" even for only a short time.

When visiting someone who is sick, here are some suggestions that may help both the visitor and the patient.

Before visiting the patient, phone ahead to let him or her know you are coming. That is just plain common sense. Your friend or loved one will appreciate you finding out a convenient time to visit. Some times a patient has had too many visitors, has gone through painful treatments or just needs to nap. If the person is sick at home and being cared for by a caregiver, knowing when you are coming may give that person a chance to run errands or plan for some personal time alone. At least it will give them a chance to tidy up the room or help the patient get ready for your visit. I know I have wished people had called first when I was receiving visitors, because I might not have been dressed appropriately and a robe or change of clothes would have made me more comfortable, etc.

The simple act of a phone call creates the anticipation of a visit, something to look forward to. Calling in advance also puts the patient in charge. Being sick often results in a forced passivity. When you phone and ask if it is all right to visit, the patient is able to exercise some control in whether they feel up to visitors at that time.

Do your research. If the person you are visiting is in a hospital or rehab facility, then call ahead to see when visiting hours are. Ask if there are any other restrictions. Some facilities do not allow children or pets. Find out if it is all right for the patient to receive flowers or food of any kind. You do not want to bring your friend's favorite brand of chocolate, only to find out that they are on a special diet and can not eat it right now. Inquire as to what you are allowed to bring. Can the patient eat food brought in from the outside? Can she have flowers etc? Some patients are very sensitive to perfumes or smells, so check if this is the case and leave those types of things at home. The most important point here is to ask questions.

Don't plan on a long visit. Hospital patients have a busy schedule and sick people often tire easily. It is better to visit briefly but more often, than to visit once for a long time. When the patient tires, leave courteously with a promise to return another time or to call. Stay long enough to put a smile on their face, but not too long as to see their smile tire. Most people would rather have many visits, then one long dragged out one.

This should also help to put the visitor at ease. If you plan on a short visit, you do not need to worry about what to say or how to "fill up" time. A 15-20 minute visit is just long enough to say hello, catch up, help out and leave. You can play a game for 20 minutes, or take a walk. Stay as long as the patient wants.

What to Bring

It's best to bring as little as you can to the hospital. You will need:

- bathrobe and slippers (put your name on each item); most hospitals provide special hospital bed clothes
- comfortable clothes to wear home (they may be the same clothes you wore to the hospital)
- toothbrush, toothpaste, shampoo, comb and brush, deodorant, and razor
- your hearing aids or glasses
- a little cash (not more than $10) to buy newspapers or magazines

Make sure you bring your health insurance card and updated information about:

- past illnesses and surgeries
- your medicines, including prescription and over-the-counter drugs
- your allergies

- names and telephone numbers (home and business) to contact in an emergency
- Bring the patient a small gift. This is not about money spent- the gift can be something you made, like a card. Let's face facts, we all like receiving gifts, especially when we are not feeling our best. A newspaper or magazine can reinforce a sense of connection to the outside world. Besides being pretty- flowers, plants or cards leave tangible evidence of the visit. I remember when I was in the hospital I spent hours looking at my "wall of cards" and reminisced about who came to visit me. It always brought a smile to my face, even if it was days after the person left.

Bring something that can be a distraction after you have left. Crossword puzzle books, reading books, even lotto scratch off's. Anything that they can easily do on their own. Many places do not allow visitors after certain hours, so your gift will help with the boredom at night and be a welcome relief.

What to Leave Home

Leave jewelry (including wedding rings, earrings, and watches), extra cash, credit cards, and checkbooks at home, or have a family member or friend keep them for you. Don't bring electric shavers, hair dryers, curling irons, or other equipment.

When it comes to visiting patients in a hospital, even the most mannered one of us finds himself/ herself at a loss. It's another thing to meet an ailing person at his/her house, but completely different to pay a visit in the hospital. Sometimes, even with best intentions at heart, we fail to please the patient. This is because many of us are still lacking the good bed-side manners. In case you want to explore proper etiquette for visiting hospital patients, the do's and don'ts given here are what you should keep in mind.

IMPORTANT TIPS FOR HOSPITAL VISITS

Wear Proper Clothing

When you are visiting a patient, remember the reason while dressing up as well. Never ever wear flashy or gaudy clothes to the hospital. Rather, you should dress up in comfortable, plain-colored clothes, in colors that are soothing to the eyes. Use minimal or no makeup and no perfumes please!

Follow Visiting Hours

As soon as people hear about a friend or relative being at hospital, they rush to it without realizing that they might be disturbing the patient. Before paying a visit to the hospital, make yourself aware of the official visiting hours. At the same time, always inform either the patient or his/her relatives about your visit.

Bring a Suitable Present

Flowers and books are the usual gifts that people bring for patients. However, you need to be sure that the gift is suitable as well. For instance, it's improper to gift a book to a person who recently have gone through eye-operation or flowers to a person who is allergic to pollen. While choosing the gift, keep in mind the occasion and likes-dislikes of the patient.

Avoid Taking Eatables

Most of the hospitals provide food for the patients and it's not suitable to take along any eatables. As it is, generally, the patients are kept on special diet and interfering with that may harm the patient. However, you might ask the doctor if it is okay for you to bring fruits the next time.

Always Be Ready To Help

You are visiting a patient, who has undergone great discomfort in the recent past and might be under great pain right now also. So, be ready for a little discomfort. You should also show your eagerness to be of help. Ask if you could help the patients or his/her family members in any way, but don't stress too much.

Don't Talk Or Laugh Loudly

It's good that you try to take out the gloom from the, otherwise, depressive hospital atmosphere, say by cracking a subtle joke. However, talking and laughing as if you're in a party is not acceptable. You may even end up disturbing the other patients. You should talk in a low, but audible voice.

Prepare the Conversation

If you're visiting someone you don't know too well, prepare the topics of conversation beforehand. Weave the conversation around safe topic, like games, entertainment, etc. If you're visiting a colleague, avoid talking about work as it may stress them. Also, avoid talking about parties or the fun he/she is missing.

Talk About Positive Things

Generally, the hospital environment is full of gloom. Try to lift up the depressing environment by talking about positive things. Instead of ranting on, listen to the patient if they want to describe his/her woes and pains. Act sympathetic and tolerant and try to cheer him/her up.

No "Favorite" Doctor Suggestion

Don't deter the faith of the patient in his/her doctor. It's not ethical on your part and neither is it advisable. You entitled to make a suggestion only if the patient specifically expresses his/her wish to change the existing one.

Don't Stay Too Long

Patients are in hospital because they are ill, so they are prone to get tired easily. Therefore, take the cue and don't stay long. Five to ten minutes are generally enough. However, if it's a near relative or close friend, you can stay longer.

No Sitting On Patient's Bed

Never every on the patient's bed, while visiting him/her, even if there are no chairs available. Besides cramping the patient, it might also lead to infection and harm him/her.

Avoid Bringing Small Children

Hospital is no place for children. If you have small kids, arrange a babysitter for the time you want to spend at hospital. Avoid taking them to hospital as they are susceptible to germs and might also start acting fussy, thus hampering your visit.

Admission

Once your hospital stay is planned, many hospitals have a staff member call to ask pre-admissions questions over the phone. Then, when you go to the hospital, many of the forms are already filled in.

Your first stop at the hospital is the admitting office. You will sign forms that:

- give the hospital details about yourself, your doctor, and your insurance
- explain your surgery, test, or procedure
- give your okay for the medical staff to treat you

You also will be asked about advance directives (see section below on Patient Rights). If you don't have health insurance, talk with the admissions staff about other payment methods and sources of financial aid.

A hospital bracelet will be put on your wrist by the admissions staff and checked by nurses. Look at your bracelet to make sure your information is correct.

Hospital Staff

While you are in the hospital, there may be many people who take care of you.

- Doctors are in charge of your overall care. The doctor in charge may be your primary doctor (the doctor you see outside the hospital), a specialist on the hospital staff, or a hospitalist who is trained to take care of you while you are in the hospital.
- Nurses - Many kinds of nurses can take care of you. For example, registered nurses can give medicines, licensed practical nurses can help feed you, and nurse's aides can help with personal care.
- Respiratory therapists prevent and treat breathing problems. They teach exercises that help avoid lung infections after surgery.
- Technicians can take blood or perform tests such as x-rays.
- Physical therapists show you how to build muscle, increase flexibility, and improve coordination.
- Occupational therapists work with you to restore, maintain, or improve the ability to perform every day tasks like cooking, eating, bathing, or dressing.
- Dietitians can plan menus including special meals and teach you how to have well-balanced meals at home.
- Clinical pharmacists may be consulted about the medicines you take.
- Social workers assist you and your family. They can help find home-care, rehabilitation, social services, long-term care, and support groups.

Inside the Hospital

Hospitals have many patient-care areas. The intensive care unit (also called the ICU) has special equipment and staff to care for very ill patients. Coronary care units (CCUs) give intensive medical care to patients with heart disease. In both the ICU and CCU, visiting hours are very limited. Often only family members are allowed to see patients. Surgery is done in the operating room (OR). After an operation, patients are cared for in the recovery room until they are ready to move to their hospital rooms.

Safety Tips

Because you may feel weak or tired, here are some safety tips to follow.

- If you are told to stay in bed, use the call bell or button when you need help.
- Use the controls to lower your bed before getting in or out.
- Sit on the edge of the bed for a minute or so before standing up.
- Watch out for the wires and tubes that may be around your bed.
- Try to keep the things you need within easy reach.
- Only take medicines given to you by nurses. Don't take medicine you brought from home without your doctor's permission.
- Hold on to grab bars for support when getting in and out of the bathtub or shower and when using the toilet.

GERIATRIC EVALUATION

Older people may have health problems that make it hard for them to live on their own after they leave the hospital. In some hospitals, a team that includes a doctor, nurse, and social worker takes care of the special needs of older patients. This team also may include other specialists and therapists.

The team performs a careful exam, called a geriatric assessment, to learn about the patient's physical and mental health, family life, income, living arrangements, access to community services, and ability to perform daily tasks. The team checks for health problems and makes a plan to help older patients get the health care and social services they need after they go home.

For Family and Caregivers

A hospital stay can be very hard for older people. Often the strange routine and lack of sleep can cause confusion. Family and caregivers may be the first to notice these changes. Families should talk to a doctor if they see any confusion.

Ask Questions

During your hospital stay, you may have questions about what's happening. You may want to ask your doctor or nurse:

- What will this test tell you? Why is it needed and when will you know the results?
- What treatment is needed and how long will it last?
- What are the benefits and risks of treatment?
- When can I go home?
- When I go home, will I have to change my regular activities or my diet?
- How often will I need checkups?
- Is any other follow-up needed?
- Who should I call if I have other questions?

Patient Rights

Before you go to the hospital, you might want to think about writing an advance directive. An advance directive says what medical treatment you want if you can't speak for yourself. It also lets you name who you want to make your medical decisions. Two common kinds of advance directives are:

- living will
- durable power of attorney for health care

In a living will, you list the kind of medical care you want (or don't want); it's called a living will because it takes effect while you are still alive.

In a durable power of attorney for health care, you name someone else (a family member or friend, for example) to make your medical decisions if you are unable to make them for yourself. You also can list any treatment you don't want.

If you have an advance directive, bring a copy of it with you to the hospital. Make sure your doctor has a copy and check to make sure your wishes are part of your medical records. If you have a durable power of attorney for health care, be sure to give a copy to the person you've chosen to act on your behalf.

Going Home

When you are ready to go home, you'll get discharge plans from the medical team and a release form from the hospital business office. Sometimes people go from the hospital to a rehabilitation (rehab) center before going home. The social worker can help you go home or arrange admission to a rehab center.

In An Emergency

In a medical emergency, every second counts! You may have severe pain, a bad injury, or sudden serious illness. In such a life-threatening emergency, seek medical help right away by calling 911. Be sure to tell the operator your problem and the address where you are calling from.

You should always carry the following information:

- doctor's name and phone number

- family members' names and phone numbers
- medicines you take, including prescription and over-the-counter drugs
- medicines you are allergic to
- health insurance information and policy number

If you have a medical problem such as epilepsy or diabetes, you should wear an ID bracelet or carry an ID card to let rescue workers and hospital staff know about these conditions.

Trauma Center

This article is about the type of hospital. For the video game series, see Trauma Center (series).

A trauma center is a hospital equipped to provide comprehensive emergency medical services to patients suffering traumatic injuries. Trauma centers grew into existence out of the realization that traumatic injury is a disease process unto itself requiring specialized and experienced multidisciplinary treatment and specialized resources.

According to the CDC, injuries are the leading cause of death for children and adults ages 1-44.

The leading causes of trauma are motor vehicle accidents, falls, and assaults.

In the United States, a hospital can receive Trauma Center verification by meeting specific criteria established by the American College of Surgeons (ACS) and passing a site review by the Verification Review Committee. Official designation as a Trauma Center is determined by individual state law provisions. Trauma centers vary in their specific capabilities and are identified by "Level" designation: Level-I (Level-1) being the highest, to Level-III (Level-3) being the lowest (some states have five designated levels, in which case Level-V (Level-5) is the lowest).

Higher levels of trauma centers will have trauma surgeons available, including those trained in such specialties as Neurosurgery and Orthopedic surgery as well as highly sophisticated medical diagnostic equipment. Lower levels of trauma centers may only be able to provide initial care and stabilization of a traumatic injury and arrange for transfer of the victim to a higher level of trauma care.

The operation of a trauma center is extremely expensive. Some areas are under-served by trauma centers because of this expense (for example, Harborview Medical Center in Seattle is the only Level I trauma center to serve the entirety of Washington, Idaho, Montana, and Alaska). As there is no way to schedule the need for emergency services, patient traffic at trauma centers can vary widely. A variety of different methods have been developed for dealing with this.

A trauma center will often have a helipad for receiving patients that have been airlifted to the hospital. In many cases, persons injured in remote areas and transported to a distant trauma center by helicopter can receive faster and better medical care than if they had been transported by ground ambulance to a closer hospital that does not have a designated trauma center. The trauma level certification can directly affect the patient's outcome and determine if the patient needs to be transferred to a higher level trauma center.

HISTORY

The concept of a trauma center was developed at the University of Maryland, Baltimore, in the 1960s and 1970s by heart surgeon and shock researcher R Adams Cowley, who founded what became the Shock Trauma Center in Baltimore, Maryland, in 1961. Cook County Hospital in Chicago, Illinois claims to be the first trauma center (opened in 1966) in the United States. Dr. David R Boyd interned at

Cook County Hospital from 1963-1964 before being drafted into the United States Army. Upon his release from the Army, Dr. Boyd became the first shock-trauma fellow at the Shock Trauma Center from 1967-1968. Dr. Boyd returned to Cook County Hospital, where he went on to serve as resident director of the Cook County Trauma Unit (www.cookcountytrauma.com).

DEFINITIONS IN THE UNITED STATES

In the United States, trauma centers are ranked by the American College of Surgeons (ACS), from Level I (comprehensive service) to Level III (limited-care). The different levels refer to the kinds of resources available in a trauma center and the number of patients admitted yearly. These are categories that define national standards for trauma care in hospitals. Level I and Level II designations are also given adult and or pediatric designations. Additionally, some states have their own trauma-center rankings separate from the ACS. These levels may range from Level I to Level IV. Some hospitals are less-formally designated Level V.

The ACS does not officially designate hospitals as trauma centers. Numerous U.S. hospitals that are not verified by ACS claim Trauma Center designation. Most states have legislation which determines the process for designation of Trauma Centers within their state. The ACS describes that responsibility as "a geopolitical process by which empowered entities, government or otherwise, are authorized to designate." The ACS's self-appointed mission is limited to confirming and reporting on any given hospital's ability to comply with the ACS standard of care known as Resources for Optimal Care of the Injured Patient.

The Trauma Information Exchange Program (TIEP) is a program of the American Trauma Society in collaboration with the Johns Hopkins Center for Injury Research and Policy and is funded by the Centers for Disease Control and Prevention. TIEP maintains an inventory of trauma centers in the U.S., collects data and develops information related to the causes, treatment and outcomes of injury, and facilitates the exchange of information among trauma care institutions, care providers, researchers, payers and policy makers.

Level I

A Level I trauma center provides the highest level of surgical care to trauma patients. Being treated at a Level 1 Trauma Center increases a seriously injured patient's chances of survival by an estimated 20 to 25 percent. It has a full range of specialists and equipment available 24 hours a day and admits a minimum required annual volume of severely injured patients. A Level I trauma center is required to have a certain number of surgeons, emergency physicians and anesthesiologists on duty 24 hours a day at the hospital, an education program, preventive and outreach programs. Key elements include 24-hour in-house coverage by general surgeons and prompt availability of care in varying specialties-such as orthopedic surgery, neurosurgery, plastic surgery (plastic surgeons often take calls for hand and facial injuries, fixing both the bone and soft tissue of these specialized regions), anesthesiology, emergency medicine, radiology, internal medicine, oral and maxillofacial surgery, and critical care-which are needed to adequately respond and care for various forms of trauma that a patient may suffer. Additionally, a Level I center has a program of research, is a leader in trauma education and injury prevention, and is a referral resource for communities in nearby regions.

Level II

A Level II trauma center works in collaboration with a Level I center. It provides comprehensive trauma care and supplements the clinical expertise of a Level I institution. It provides 24-hour availability of all essential specialties, personnel, and equipment. Minimum volume requirements may depend on local conditions. These institutions are not required to have an ongoing program of research or a surgical residency program.

Level III

A Level III trauma center does not have the full availability of specialists, but does have resources for emergency resuscitation, surgery, and intensive care of most trauma patients. A Level III center has transfer agreements with Level I or Level II trauma centers that provide back-up resources for the care of exceptionally severe injuries, Example: Rural or Community hospitals.

Level IV

A Level IV trauma center exists in some states where the resources do not exist for a Level III trauma center. It provides initial evaluation, stabilization, diagnostic capabilities, and transfer to a higher level of care. It may also provide surgery and critical-care services, as defined in the scope of services for trauma care. A trauma-trained nurse is immediately available, and physicians are available upon the patient's arrival to the Emergency Department. Transfer agreements exist with other trauma centers of higher levels, for use when conditions warrant a transfer.

Level V

Provides initial evaluation, stabilization, diagnostic capabilities, and transfer to a higher level of care. May provide surgical and critical-care services, as defined in the service's scope of trauma-care services. A trauma-trained nurse is immediately available, and physicians are available upon patient arrival in the Emergency Department. If not open 24 hours daily, the facility must have an after-hours trauma-response protocol.

12

ADVERTISING POLICY FOR HEALTH TOURISM

The advertising of health tourism to Cyprus could have a knock-on effect in the quality and cost of private healthcare provided on the island, operators said at the Heathcare Business Conference in Nicosia.

One problem identified is the lack of international accreditation. Currently the accreditation position is lagging considerably in Cyprus, a situation that has been ongoing for two years despite the Health Ministry promising to co-sponsor the accreditation applications of a number of private health institutions. So far, only the Bank of Cyprus Oncology Centre in Nicosia has been accredited by CHKS and Near East University Faculty of Dentistry in Lefkosahas been accredited by JCI' although the latter is not interested in health tourism.

The conference was told that the country is owed money from EU countries that it cannot reclaim as private healthcare institutions in Cyprus which treat foreign citizens resident in Cyprus under reciprocal treatment schemes cannot secure payment for the treatment from the national governments or insurance companies in question. Nikos Maroudias of the Cyprus Health Service Promotion Board argues, "The increase in the quality standards which comes with health tourism will also benefit local patients."

The standards, service and perhaps, above all, cost of healthcare in Cyprus is deemed sufficiently competitive in the European market for the Cyprus Chamber of Commerce and Industry (CCCI) to have held a conference to promote and examine the industry. Dental treatment in Cyprus, for example, is on average about 40-50 per cent cheaper than the UK.

Manthos Mavromatis of the CCCI comments," Cyprus is in line with European standards and in a harmonised position regarding the healthcare industry, so it is useful for Europeans who wish to undergo treatment. The Health Ministry has engaged in an unforgivable delay in certifying some private healthcare institutes. We call on the ministry to certify them, so that they can get on with doing their job." The Cyprus Tourism Organisation (CTO) says there are 11 health centres yet to receive Health Ministry accreditation, where private investors have expressed an interest filed with the CTO under the Motivational Plan for the Improvement of the Tourist Product. The Cyprus Health Service Promotion Board is also pushing for accreditation.

With the economic crisis a drop in foreign custom as high as 30 per cent has been experienced by private healthcare providers on the island. This is a trend that has also been affected by cheaper alternative destinations being available for the medical tourist, such as Hungary, Bulgaria and Syria. Cyprus remains very competitive in terms of the costs involved but does need to work on remaining competitive and on lowering its prices.

After being hit by the recession and a fall in tourism numbers, one of the main hospitals in Nicosia was badly damaged by the recent storms that caused death and destruction across Europe.

ADVERTISING OPPORTUNITIES FOR MEDICAL TOURISM

The Treatment Abroad web site helps people to find information about health and medical tourism for UK citizens. Treatment Abroad and its sister site, Private

Healthcare UK, hold a commanding position on the internet search engines and directories.

Private healthcare providers attract more "referrals" (click throughs) from site listings than from search engines such as MSN, AOL, Ask Jeeves and Yell Directory. This has been confirmed from examining activity logs for our clients' sites.

Healthcare companies, healthcare services, clinics and hospital facilities outside of the UK can participate in the Treatment Abroad web site in the following ways:

- By purchasing a featured listing within our listing pages.
- By sponsoring a section of the site and perhaps providing content.
- By purchasing banner advertising on specific pages or throughout the site.
- By signing up for the Enquiry Forwarding system, and receiving enquiries for healthcare services from people who are considering travelling abroad for treatment.

Health Promotion Agency Welcomes Ban on Tobacco Advertising

The Health Promotion Agency has welcomed the decision by the Government to support a bill that will ban tobacco advertising. In Northern Ireland, there are almost 3,000 premature deaths from smoking related diseases each year. This new legislation will ban press, billboard and internet advertising of tobacco products and will also prohibit any form of marketing promotion on smoking through free distribution of tobacco products, coupons and mail shots. The bill will also stop tobacco companies sponsoring sporting and other events.

Rob Phipps, Senior Health Promotion Programme Manager, Health Promotion Agency said: "The Agency is delighted with this decision in particular the restrictions that will be placed on the display and promotion of tobacco products in shops. We know from research that one in three fifth form girls are smoking daily in Northern Ireland which is double the number of boys of the same age who smoke. We also know that the brands most heavily advertised are those most heavily smoked by children.

"Banning all forms of tobacco advertising will help reduce the number of young people who are taking up this habit at an early age and will also support those who wish to stop smoking. When this ban is in place it will be a major step towards creating our ultimate aim of an environment where non-smoking is seen as the norm," he said.

The Health Promotion Agency's 'Every cigarette is doing you damage' campaign is currently encouraging all smokers in Northern Ireland to stop.

Every person is bombarded with hundreds of advertising messages every day. These range from television commercials billboards to logos on coffee cups. Consumer studies show this adds up to an average of more than 500 messages daily.

Most of these messages are ignored. Only a few motivate a response, whether positive or negative; only a fraction result in actual purchase. This sheer message overload makes it essential for the small business owner and the Chamber of Commerce executive to be skilled in using marketing tools to increase chances of success in the travel marketplace. Members of local tourism promotion groups need an awareness of advertising options as well.

Marketing attempts to match the product with consumer preferences. A mix of messages and format are used to market your product or service: advertising is just one aspect. Advertising - along with publicity, personal selling, and incentives - is one of the major tools used to persuade the target market to buy. Advertising is defined as all nonpersonal forms of communication where paid media is used and the formal sponsor is identified. It includes many medium: newspapers, magazines, brochures, direct mail, displays, television, radio, and novelty items.

Four types of advertising-brand, information, image and reminder-begin to suggest the many purposes advertising can Brand advertising, the most common, tries to stimulate sales by building product loyalty. Brand advertising is competitive: advertisers often hype their product's advantages over their competitor's.

Information advertising highlights facts and can introduce a new product to the consumer. A new tourist destination may convey information to create awareness as much as a competitive message ("we offer a better travel experience") first entering the marketplace. Information advertising is often used where demand does not presently exist.

Advertising can enhance an organization's image in the long can also remind consumers to keep buying on a regular basis. Coca-Cola is an example of a product at this mature stage.

Five decisions must be made in selecting an advertising strategy:

- Set advertising objectives.
- Determine the advertising budget.
- Create the advertising message.
- Select the advertising media.
- Evaluate the advertising results.

This publication introduces advertising strategies that not option for your business or community. Cost is likely to be most serious constraint. However, it is important to understand the range of approaches that exist. This is particularly true given the pressures to move beyond standard forms of advertising in order to gain attention in crowded marketplace. Understanding options available to the competition can also enhance your own campaign.

Set Advertising Objectives

Advertising objectives flow from previous marketing decisions about your product, target market, image, and knowledge of the competition. Decide whether the message is persuasive, informational, image building, or a reminder. Outline exactly what you want the advertising program to accomplish. Mention a specific target market and a time frame to achieve it. The new owner of a gift shop may objective to "bring in 300 new customers from the nearby resorts within two months to introduce them new retail offerings." A rural community might target Fargo-Moorhead residents with the objective of increasing attendance at a September harvesting festival.

Determine the Advertising Budget

Options for determining an advertising budget fall into four basic categories: investment, affordable, competitive, percent of sales. The best (and least used) way to set an advertising budget is to view advertising dollars as an investment. Advertising must increase profit margins to more than offset advertising expenditures. Costs must be tied to results to avoid draining profits and reserves. Set objectives, then define the tasks required to accomplish this goal, and determine the cost of performing those tasks.

The universal advice in all business sectors is to consider advertising as a necessary expenditure, like interest payments and utilities, to assure the health of the business. It is not a luxury to be cut first when revenues decline.

What you would like to invest and what you can afford rarely match. A budget based on "what I can afford" is certainly a critical question for most in the tourism sector. However, using funds "leftover" after paying other bills makes for a very unstable and uncertain operating environment. Long-range planning is difficult. A low priority on advertising also ignores the effect of marketing on sales volume. The compromise is to work through a budget analysis by another method, and then to adjust advertising objectives if costs exceed available funds.

Private firms and communities differ so widely that it quickly becomes meaningless to compare advertising budgets. Comparison is defensive rather than aggressive. Percent of sales is often touted as a simple way to calculate advertising budgets. A fixed dollar amount is set annually based on previous sales, and then allocated to individual advertising components; for example, newspaper ads and brochures. However, there are no hard and fast rules for selecting a percentage, and this strategy ignores unexpected opportunities that could arise such as a late snowfall or a "hot" trend. Instead money is distributed on the basis of availability. A serious drawback of the percentage method is if revenues fall, you will spend less at a time when you need to devote more resources to advertising.

Investigate other resources to supplement available funds. The Minnesota Office of Tourism administers a joint venture marketing program. Advertising campaigns may be eligible for matching funds allocated on a competitive basis to any local, regional, or statewide nonprofit tourism organization formed to promote tourism. You might also be able to work out trade arrangements with the media where you exchange advertising time or space for the travel services you offer.

Create the Advertising Message

Marketing a service, like travel opportunities, is very different from selling a tangible product like a car. One fundamental difference is that tourism depends largely on the personalities of the people who deliver the travel experience - the people who meet and greet guests. It can not be controlled the way circumstances surrounding the purchase of weekly grocery items can be controlled. There are also different rewards for the consumer. Usually people vacation experiences because of emotional rewards rather than purely rational reasons. An advertising message from a creative endeavor that tries to reach a customer whose travel expectations may be complex. Travel's personal nature and emotional appeal shape the advertising message.

It is important to make key points prominent in your advertising message. Many things could be said about any product, and probably an unlimited variety for travel destinations. No ad should attempt to say it all: say a few well. To set your business or community apart, there might be times when it is appropriate to concentrate on only one feature. Talk to your guests, to the experts, and even to competitors to determine what is distinctive about your operations or offerings.

Ogilvy and Mother, a top advertising firm with many travel accounts, heads its list of suggestions on creating the advertising message with similar advice:

* Spotlight unique differences you offer.
* Facts are better than generalities. "As low as $399" is better than saying "reasonably priced."
* Don't shy away from ads with lots of text if what you have to say is important in selling your product. Image advertising is an exception to this.
* Alleviate anxiety about going to a new place. In Minnesota, travelers may be lukewarm about going to a new destination, or to the North Woods where lodging and eating are unknown.
* Use research to test daring new ideas, and don't be afraid to try. Don't follow and mimic: create and lead.
* Stress quality, quality, quality in ad appearance and content.
* Bargains are still irresistible.
* If there's news -"the first," "the only"- treat it as newsand feature it prominently in the ad. The Minnesota Explorer

newspaper of the Minnesota Office of Tourism uses this strategy.

* Use coupons as more than just clip- outs in one corner of the ad. Make the coupon the focus of your ad, or write more information on the coupon. Often, the coupon is the only thing that gets read. (Don't forget to code coupons by address for evaluation.)
* Photographs gain a lot of attention and should be captioned (from Reilly 1980).

Advertisements are evaluated with the AIDA principle attention, interest, desire, and action. First be sure that potential guests look at an ad, and then that they are interested enough to read on. A good ad will create a desire or need for the product and motivate action.

Select the Advertising Media

Media selection means finding the most cost-effective way to deliver the message to the desired audience. Reach, frequency, and impact are key concepts in selecting the combination of media used. each is the number of people exposed to your message. Frequency is the number of times they are exposed to the message. Impact is the quality of the exposure in terms of consumer response.

Remember that advertising deals with cumulative effects. Visitor response usually comes from a variety of media used long time span. A wide variety of options exist for timing your media campaign. You can send out your advertising message continuously, in concentrated small "bursts," or at regular intervals. Remember that vacation decisions are usually made well in advance of actual travel. Coupled with media production schedules set well on advance, a very long planning horizon becomes necessary for media buys.

Know your target audience's media habits. Consider the type message you want to convey. For example, an upcoming special event needs the immediacy of television and radio coverage. Yet, a detailed tour package is best presented in written format.

Advertising costs are a major consideration. Cost per thousand (CPM) is a useful concept in judging alternative media strategies. Cost per thousand is defined as the cost to deliver one full page black and white ad to 1 ,000 households. It is computed as:

Cost of one page x 1 ,000 = CPM

Circulation

Although primarily used to compare magazine rates, it can be applied to television and radio if you change the formula slightly:

Newspapers

Newspapers contain both classified and display advertising. Classifieds charge by the inch, word, or line. Most of the tourism industry finds display ads, billed on the basis of the column inch, more effective. A column inch spans a single column about 2 inches wide and 1 inch deep.

Advertisers can buy any portion of a page measured in column inches. Typically you can specify where you would like the ad to appear (travel, entertainment, sports), but particular ad positions are not guaranteed.

Circulation largely determines price. There are usually discounts for frequent advertisers. Newspapers will often provide preliminary consultation on putting together an ad campaign at no additional cost. Extra charges may be assessed for color and any staff help provided on artwork, layout, and type setting.

Many Chambers of Commerce encourage local tourism businesses to advertise cooperatively under a banner headline naming the community to gain more visibility for one destination. The Star Tribune: Newspaper of the Twin Cities runs an Explore Minnesota banner each Sunday in the travel section. Some Chamber executives suggest placing an occasionally in the local area to increase community support and visibility for tourism.

Magazines

Magazine advertising is a lot like newspaper advertising - flat, one-time rates - with several exceptions. Magazines sell a portion of the page, in full, half, quarter, 1/8, etc. increments. So there are limits on how you use space. Additional charges for preferred positions include the back center spread, inside covers, and those ads placed near popular writers' columns. Normally ads to the magazine are camera-ready, meaning everything is in place to print.

Publisher's statements contain information on circulation, renewal rates, and geographic breakdown of their subscribers. When you consider circulation figures, the primary cost factor, be sure to get a breakdown on paid versus nonpaid circulation. A large percentage of complimentary subscriptions limit your ability to make generalizations about the target audience.

The rise in special interest magazines featuring certain recreation activities and hobbies (such as Canoe), geographic regions (Midwest Living), and lifestyles (Modern Maturity for retired persons) have made it easier to reach distinct market segments. Also consider magazines for the travel trade such as motorcoach tour operators, travel agents, and meeting/convention planners.

Brochures

The Minnesota Extension Service publication, "Tourism Brochures to Boost Business" discusses brochure development use of brochures in marketing.

Direct Mail

Direct mail, as the name implies, is a package of advertising materials mailed to selected target market members. Total costs are based on production, list preparation, and mailing activities. Direct mail can appear expensive at first glance, but when you consider the locate one interested customer, it can be a cost-effective strategy. There are print expenses in preparing the information to be which could include letters, brochures, catalogs, postcards, price lists, or coupons. Consider working with a local business, utility company, college, etc., to include paycheck or bill "stuffers" that highlight tourist opportunities.

A mailing list can be purchased: an industry average cost is from $40 to $70 for 1,000 names. It is impossible to overemphasize the importance of the quality of the list you The best list often is previous customers' names obtained from receipts or registers. The informal 20-80 rule in marketing states that 20 percent of your customers are apt to generate 80 percent of your business. They have introduced to the services you provide and can be the most likely prospects. The also can generate good word-of-mouth advertising. If you mail to the travel trade, keep in mind the volume of mail that travel agents and tour operators receive.

Bulk mail costs less than first class postage, but consider many people throw away bulk mail without opening it. The quality of your package can offset this tendency. Try unusual tactics to set your material apart. For example a gift; shop featuring Third Wold handicrafts mailed a letter overseas using colorful stamps of the country to reach previous customers. Include costs for return mail if provide a way for the customer to respond. There is a major time commitment in the mailing itself. Mailing houses will sort, label, stuff, and tie direct mail packages for a fee. Resorters have been using this idea for years - Christmas letters that remind past guests of great times or to book soon for the upcoming season. The idea is increasing in popularity and has year-round applicability. The community Askov had greater attendance at a local Danish celebration after sending a direct mail piece to members of the Danish-American Society.

Lansboro sent out a glossy detailing Christmas activities in town to former guest at lodging establishments. The Winona Chamber of Commerce has mailed a brochure on birdwatching in the region to members of the Audubon Society in the Upper Midwest.

Outdoor Advertising

Billboards are the most common form of outdoor advertising, and can be very effective is used properly. Think of the impact of the Arizona billboards that go up along the freeway near downtown Minneapolis in winter. Conversely, a Minnesota lake scene in downtown Phoenix in August could have a similar effect. Keep the message simple. Billboard strategy is based on size, traffic volume, and type (for example, illuminated). Most companies that lease advertising prefer at least a two month contract commitment.

Outdoor advertising is usually designed to create awareness. Impulse buying is not common for travel decisions so opportunities to change a traveler's plans are great - with the exception of businesses geared to the travel transit - motels, attractions, gift chops, etc. Instead, your advertising should place the option of a future visit in the mind of the consumer. One campground on Highway 169 North, a major thoroughfare, proclaims "You'd be Here Now if You Had Chosen Us." Similarly, the Minnesota Zoo billboard campaign targets drivers who regularly use Interstate 494 and Highways 7 and 12. Another option to complement media advertising is transit advertising on buses (both inside and outside) and taxis.

Television

Advertising in prime time evening hours in 15-, 30-, 60- and even 90-second slots is most expensive in television. Match your target market with the characteristics of the people who watch the show. You can scatter television "buys" (purchase of time" across the entire time schedule, or concentrate on specific segments. Some experts advise buying television in weekly increments, contracting for so many spots of specific lengths in specific programs. Be sure to add on production costs. In major metropolitan areas, advertising agencies often handle television accounts. In smaller markets, you may be able to negotiate directly with the station.

Television is a difficult medium for many tourism industry businesses and destinations with a limited advertising budget. Your ads will be competing for attention with ads that cost hundreds of thousands of dollars to produce, and the quality differences will be noticeable. Your product must also have widespread appeal to be the most effective use of advertising dollars. Think of the flashy summertime commercials several state tourism offices and the Canadian Tourism Board have used on Minnesota stations. Canada has even developed different formats for different markets that the nightlife in the cities or the cultural heritage.

Over 350 cable systems in Minnesota offer more advertising choices. Once cable has been awarded to an area, alternatives include private-for-profit or dedicated channels. You can insert advertising to be seen only by local subscribers on major nationwide channels (for example, ESPN). The recently created Travel Channel offers opportunity to target advertising to an audience inclined to travel. Half of Travel Channel programing is produced in-house, like Arthur Frommer's "Almanac of Travel". The other 50 percent of the air time is allocated of travel packages to viewers and home shopping segments. Again, it is possible to buy local advertising inserts. Contact your local cable manager for more information.

Dedicated channels include community-access channels run by organizations such as cities or school districts. These are generally nonprofit entities, so use would be limited to Chambers of Commerce and noncommercial groups. For example, develop a program on local visitor opportunities to be viewed by hotel guests. You would pay for production costs, but not air time. Some community access channels use a tickertape format to announce upcoming.

Radio

Radio stations sell time in 10-, 30-, and 60-second blocks. time on AM stations is during the rush hour traffic to and from work, and mornings. On FM stations, evenings and weekend time slots are most valuable. There are surcharges for placement within special shows such as the morning news, weather or business reports.

Radio is a radically different format from print or television, so seek assistance in developing a script that is written for the ear. Ads voiced by well-known personalities can give radio more of a personal touch.

Radio stations have generally been more receptive to tradeouts than other media. This means the station trades air advertising time for a product it receives from you, and often used as a listener prize in radio promotions.

For example, a ski resort might trade lift tickets in exchange for its radio spots or a community could offer vacation packages.

Attention-getting radio spots can serve diverse purposes. The Lutsen-Tofte area used a three-prong approach, with radio complementing out-of-state print and billboard advertising. Battle Lake designed a last-minute radio blitz to increase attendance at an art festival from local resort guests and residents.

Specialty Advertising

Speciality advertising is used to keep present customers rather than to attract new ones. Gifts with the business or community name, logo, or slogan serve to increase goodwill and remind customers to purchase soon. Calendars, stickers

(Yes Virginia, There is a Sleepy Eye, Minnesota), T-shirts, matchbooks, coffee cups, and posters are in this category. The Explore Minnesota sure packets and soap maintain public awareness of Minnesota as a travel destination.

Miscellaneous Advertising

Consider placing a listing, or ad in the Yellow Pages. Travelers often make accommodation choices from a local phone book. Phone directories for large metropolitan areas are also an option for major lodging facilities and attractions; match your market profile.

Mini-attractions such as golf courses and community events can use posters as a way to get information out to visitors they stop or stay - gas stations, resorts, grocery stores, etc.

Some General Media Strategies

Know your target market well. When you approach the media, an audience profile. For example, National Geographic Traveler publishes a subscriber study outlining income, occupation, age, martial status, education, and residence. Spend your media dollars in a format that most closely matches the market segment you want to reach.

Salespeople for the media also have rate cards with basic costs for print and media prices. Resource books like Standard Rate and Data Service (SRDA) also carry this information, but are not likely to be as current. These books are available in public and business libraries.

Quantity purchases of time or line space save money. One way to cut costs is run of station (ROS) arrangement. The broadcast company places your ad in the time slots available; you monitor the actual placement. A reputable company will give you a mix of good, high visibility slots and weaker positions. Costs are lower because you loose control over the actual ad placement.

Other Advertising Outlets

Two common outlets where a variety of advertising methods are used are trade shows and travel information centers. Trade shows are actually a form of personal selling where you meet with potential customers, but advertising material supports the face-to-face activities. Likewise, travel information centers rely both on one-on-one contact and "take along" advertising pieces.

Trade shows are special interest meetings where the general (sports shows) or travel industry representatives convene (American Bus Association for example) to gather information about travel destinations and businesses. In evaluating this advertising option, include exhibit fees, travel, and per diem expenses, as well as literature costs as direct expenditures. The challenge is to select display literature and giveaway materials to be cost-effective. One way to control costs might be to hand out request cards returned by mail in order to receive expensive promotional pieces.

Public travel information centers display community and regional tourism brochures. Check with their staff about the type of inquiries they receive before sending large quantities. At the local level, many visitor centers will also display materials for private businesses that are members of an association. Long-range plans for some centers include use of video technology.

There are also private firms that contract to do private advertising displays at travel information centers, rest stops and airports. Arrangements include backlit panels, unmanned kiosks, and phone boards with toll-free phones. Community cooperative ads are also available to smaller towns. Private sector businesses advertise on one panel, with a "free space" for a nonprofit community attraction. Contact account representatives with these companies for further information.

Evaluate the Advertising Results

Advertisements can be evaluated in terms of communication effects as well as sales impacts. In the travel industry, it is common for destinations to do image adverting simply to gain awareness. Evaluation of image advertising involves series of tests before and after viewing an ad to learn how well potential customers recognize and recall the message.

Sales effect is measured by tracking inquires, booking and spending from coded advertisements. The Minnesota Extension publication, "Cost Comparison Methods to Evaluate Your Tourism Advertising Campaign" outlines methods to figure the return on your investment. Don't guess; spend your advertising dollars where your research shows they have an impact.

In planning an overall marketing campaign, advertising usually gets most cf the attention. Advertising is a very public, very persuasive tool when used on a repeat basis. But advertising is also an impersonal one-way form of communication. Advertising should be integrated with other marketing methods - publicity, personal selling, and incentives - to get the message across.

Checklist

To work through an update of your advertising plan, use the following checklist to summarize each step. Your overall marketing plan - situation analysis, product identification, target market selection, objectives - provides a framework for these decisions.

1. Have I set objectives for my advertising campaign?

* target market(s)?
* time frame?
* number of bookings, inquires, etc.?

* type of advertising (brand, image, information, reminder)?

2. What is my overall advertising budget?

3. What do I want to say in the advertising?

* image?
* main point(s)?
* slogan?

4. Does the ad message follow AIDA principles (attract, interest, desire, action)?

5. For each of the advertising components used, what is the reach, frequency, impact, and cost?

* newspapers * magazines
* brochures * direct mail
* outdoor advertising
* television, including cable channels
* radio
* speciality advertising

6. What is my strategy for travel information centers and trade shows?

7. How does the mix of advertising selected work together?

8. Is there a new advertising method I want to try? (How will I evaluate effectiveness?)

9. Have I worked with each medium for quantity discounts or trades?

10. Are any outside funding sources available?

11. Is an evaluation system in place to track resuls

from each component?

Resources

Travel and Tourism Marketing Techniques, 1980. Robert T. Reilly. Wheaton, IL; Meston House, 200 pp. Although written specifically for travel agencies, this book provides overview of the media selection process.

Foodservice/Hospitality Advertising and Promotion. 1982. Leon Gottlieb. Indianapolis, IN: Bobbs-Merrill Educational Publishing. 363 pp. -Marketing planning for restaurants and hotels.

13

HEALTH TOURISM IN DEVELOPING COUNTRIES

Asia's cultural diversity, perfect beaches and fabulous cuisines mixed with a pinch of Oriental mysticism have long drawn tourists from around the world. Recently, many of the region's top tourist destinations have added a new ingredient into the mix: health tourism.

"People have been travelling to faraway places in the quest for better health for millenniums, yet Asia's top tourist destinations are just rediscovering the potential of health tourism," said Raymond Yeung, an assistant research professor in Health Economics and Policy with the University of Hong Kong.

Medical tourism is increasingly becoming popular and competitions is growing among choices for global community. Malaysia is certainly the best and the most favorable destination in view of, why people choose medical tourism. Affordable costs for procedures, abundance of choices for tourism and accommodation. English speaking staff and Malaysian public. Excellent medical staff, and top class international hospitals with careful and strict accreditation system.

Medical tourism is carefully governed and watched by government to safe guard the rights of patients and tourists.

A very loving general population of Malaysia and always warm welcoming to tourists and guests. Excellent government facilities for medical tourists, by granting extended long stay facilities. A medical tourism guests has unending choices to make which puts Malaysia as the top destination in medical tourism.

Health tourism, or more broadly, health tourism, refers to the increasing tendency among people living where medical services are either very expensive or not available to travel overseas in search of more affordable health options, often packaged with tourist attractions.

The development is being touted as the "next big thing" in the travel industry, but in reality, people have been travelling to far-off lands to improve their health for centuries.

As far back as 3,000 BC, people with eye problems made pilgrimage to Tell Brak, Syria, where healing deities were said to perform miracles. Ancient Roman spas that were believed to cure an endless list of ailments still offer hope and relief to bathers today.

The World Tourism Organization includes the following in its definition of medical tourism: medical care, sickness and well-being, rehabilitation and recuperation.

Health tourism covers the whole spectrum of services that promote physical well-being. They range from beautiful holiday packages bundled with everything from spas to cosmetic treatments to cardiovascular surgery, and from diagnostic services to rehabilitative Chinese herbal treatments.

However, experts say not all medical services are exportable. In fact, patients are advised not to travel if they have a fever or symptoms of upper respiratory tract illnesses.

In countries like Malaysia and Thailand, medical tourism is built upon the proposition that foreign patients are able to enjoy a combination of sunshine and health promotion.

Hong Kong's health care advantages, combined with hospitality, seamless and integrated services, access to telecom and Internet services, tourist attractions, etc, provide a very tempting package, said Yeung.

"Medical tourists" will not only benefit the health sector. As they will usually be travelling with a companion, and most likely have a sizable disposable income, their shopping, dining and sightseeing excursions will benefit the whole economy, Yeung said.

Starting at the end of February, Hong Kong's Hong Thai Travel, in co-operation with Quality HealthCare, began offering health care for the tourists from the Chinese mainland, who are allowed to visit Hong Kong under the individual travellers scheme.

"We focus on offering such services to Mainlanders because we realize a lot of them are very interested in check-ups and other health care services available in Hong Kong," said Julie Chow, at Quality HealthCare.

MEDICAL TOURISM IN BRAZIL

Brazil's health system is one of the world's largest, comprising an estimated 16,000 facilities, including clinics, hospitals and local health centers that are staffed by more than 200,000 qualified physicians. The country provides some of the most advanced medical care that you'll find globally, and treatment is among the cheapest.

In recent years, the devaluation of Brazil's currency against the US dollar has made the country an excellent choice for low-cost, high-quality medical treatment for foreigners. As a result, Brazil's international reputation in the medical tourism sphere is growing.

In particular, Brazil has become world-famous for its cosmetic and plastic surgery procedures. The well-to-do have been visiting Brazil for procedures for years in order to maintain their youthful appearance and their anonymity while recuperating on Rio's fabulous beaches. With the devaluation of the currency, these procedures are now within the means of many more people.

More hospitals in Brazil have received accreditation by the Joint Commission on the Accreditation of Hospitals than in any country other than the US, and rates are among the best in Latin America. In addition to the excellent medical facilities, the country boasts many attractions that appeal to medical tourists who are interested in experiencing the culture, recuperating on a beach or taking in the many natural wonders.

INTERNATIONAL TRADE IN MEDICAL SERVICE

Patients all over the countries especially western are increasingly travelling to developing countries for health care and developing countries are increasingly offering their skills and facilities to paying foreign customers. This international trade in medical services has huge economic potential for developing countries and serious implications for health care across the globe. The potential is explored in this chapter through analysis of the market for medical tourism and identification of its link to economic growth.

Instead, it is successful only in countries with economic and political advantages that enable them to navigate around international and domestic obstacles to trade in medical services. It is also suggested that a successful medical tourism industry, when coupled with cooperation between the private and public sectors, may lead to public health improvements in developing countries.

Medical Tourism in Thailand

Thailand is leading Asia as a medical tourism destination. Medical tourism in Thailand is booming;

pushing other nations down the list. The number of medical tourists that come in Thailand has been steadily increasing since the early 2000's. This has resulted in the country taking its place on the top of the global medical tourism market.

The major reasons that have enabled Thailand to dominate this growing market are: the low cost of medical treatment, the quality treatment provided by hospitals and private clinics, and the highly developed tourism industry.

Thailand's Healthcare System

There are approximately 400 hospitals in Thailand offering advance healthcare services. The country takes pride in having the largest private hospital in Asia, as well as having the first Asian hospital to receive the ISO 9001 certification and JCI accreditation.

To date, 8 hospitals in Thailand have been accredited by the JCI:

Bumrungrad International, Bangkok Hospital, Bangkok Hospital Pattaya, Bangkok Hospital Phuket, BNH Hospital, Samitivej Srinakarin, Samitivej Sriracha, and Samitivej Sukhumvit Hospitals.

Thailand's Medical tourism industry is largely driven by private hospitals. Thai doctors are attracted to the international hospitals as they can earn as much as 70% more than in the public hospitals.

Leading the list are the Bumrungrad International Hospital, Bangkok Hospital Group, and Samitivej Hospitals. These hospitals are widely becoming renowned globally.

They are known to cater mostly to foreign patients and have been actively seeking medical tourists since 2004 or earlier. Around 30-50% of the patients in these hospitals are foreigners, due to the fact that, to a greater extent, they find the hospitals cheaper than that of their home countries. However, most Thai locals still find the prices in these hospitals too costly.

Top Hospitals for Medical Tourism in Thailand

Bumrungrad International

Bumrungrad International is known to have excellent facilities for medical tourists. The hospital has treated over 420,000 international patients in 2008, (including expatriates and medical tourists) from 190 countries worldwide (3). It attracts more foreign patients than any other hospital in the world. Over half of the hospital's doctors have international training and/or board certification, including 200 who are US board certified.

Bangkok Hospital Group

The Bangkok Hospital Group is a leading group of hospitals with specialized services for overseas patients. It has a network of 15 hospitals scattered all over Thailand. The Bangkok International Hospital in Bangkok tops the list. It has an International Medical Center which caters especially for medical tourists, and is completely employed with multilingual interpreters. It even has a Japanese Medical Centre with Japanese speaking physicians and nurses.

Samitivej Hospitals

The Samitivej Hospitals are a well known chain in Thailand. The group has expanded and developed world class healthcare facilities, and has become recognized by medical tourists from all over the world. It has been collecting many prestigious awards in recent years, including 3 JCI accredited hospitals. Samitivej Hospitals are equipped with advanced medical equipment that compares to the leading hospitals in the North America and Europe.

Browse our list of medical tourism hospitals in Thailand.

Common Procedures done by Medical Tourists in Thailand

Healthcare services and treatments offered by the hospitals and clinics in Thailand cover an extensive list. The procedures medical tourists come for varies diversely diversely. Nevertheless, the popular treatments include the following:

Cosmetic / plastic Surgeries

Every aesthetic procedure in Thailand costs only a small fraction as compared to what patients in US and UK would pay back home. Yet, the standard of service and treatment is usually high.

Dental Procedures

From routine checkups to the most complicated dental surgeries, many Thai dental clinics and hospitals are well equipped and employed to execute a complete range of dental treatments. The costs are also comparatively low and the standards are international.

Medical Check-up Programs

Medical check-up programs are a growing trend in the global medical tourism market. These programs are recommended for everyone, and the frequency would depend on the patient's age and condition. They are particularly recommended for patients in their 40's or 50's. Every major hospital in Thailand has inclusive check-up packages.

Cardiac Procedures

Many hospitals in Thailand, including the Bangkok Heart Hospital, have cardiac surgery centers. Procedures carried out in Thailand include heart bypass, angioplasty, and heart valve replacement, among others.

Orthopedic Surgery

Foreign patients fly Thailand to get different kinds of orthopedic procedures. Many orthopedic surgeons in Thailand have been trained overseas and equipment used for the procedures are assured to be modern and innovative, including the Computer Assisted Surgery (CAS) Micro Invasive Surgery (MAS). Common orthopedic surgeries that take place in Thailand are hip and knee replacement, as well as spine surgeries.

Low Cost of Medical Treatments

The treatment costs in Thailand amount to only a fraction to that of their counterparts in most Western countries. The prices for treatment are usually between 20-50% lower than that of an equivalent treatment in the West. This low cost leaves the medical tourist a budget for recuperation and even recreation.

High Quality Healthcare Services

In recent years, Thailand's private sector has established a growing number of medical facilities that can be compared side by side with leading hospitals worldwide. The country has over 30 hospitals that cater to medical tourists, as well as numerous dental and cosmetic clinics and other medical and alternative medicine centers. Hospitals in Thailand that have the JCI accreditation amount to 8, and all hospitals in Thailand are licensed by the country's Ministry of Public Health.

Physicians in Thailand are also highly educated and trained. Many of them hold professional certifications obtained in the US and/or Europe. In Bumrungrad for example, approximately 200 doctors are US board certified and 400 were trained in Western hospitals (5).

Highly Developed Tourism Infrastructure

Thailand is among the top holiday destinations in the world, being a paradise of inviting beaches and nature's best scenes. The country has a rich culture with a splendid cuisine, and people are friendly and accommodating to foreigners. If it were not for the integration of these tourism strengths to the medical service sector, the status of Thailand's medical tourism would not be so well developed. Being a major tourist destination, service is one of the top factors that contributed to the industry's success. Thai people strive to give their best in rendering services to their country's visitors. Whereas, foreigners are glad to receive the same quality of service be it in the hotel or in the hospital.

Cons

Lack of Primary Healthcare System

Despite the fact that many doctors in Thailand have studied and received training in the US or UK, most of them are specialists. Unfortunately, the healthcare system of Thailand relies heavily on specialized medicine. This means that common minor ailments or several medical problems all at once, are hard for a specialist to pinpoint. If an underlying symptom is unknown, general medicine or internists would be the best option.

Some Doctors are Employed Part Time

There are doctors in Thailand, including physicians and surgeons in different specialties, who

work under various hospitals. They tend to juggle schedules between different hospitals all over Thailand, sometimes even having their own private clinical services somewhere. When choosing a doctor or surgeon, make sure you know their schedule in advance, and demand to get the attention you need before paying the money. Comparatively though, doctors and medical staff in Thailand are much more attentive than doctors in the West.

Lack of Emergency Transport Facilities

While most hospitals have ambulatory services, there is still a lack of transport in case of emergency 'call outs'. This specifically refers to air transport, as alternative to land transport in cases of heavy traffic or immediacy of need.

Potential of Health Tourism in Malaysia

Malaysia is fast becoming a strong competitor in the global health and medical tourism sector. Given the potential of health tourism as a foreign exchange earner, the government has taken a series of proactive measures to enhance Malaysia as a preferred health tourism destination.

Health tourism in Malaysia consists of two main categories which are medical tourism and wellness programme. Patients can opt for medical treatments in one of our internationally recognised hospitals, and stay on during the convalescence or recovery period. Or they can come for a holiday by exploring the various forms of wellness programmes that are available in Malaysia.

Competitive medical fees and modern medical facilities are two vital factors that make Malaysia a popular destination among health tourists. Patients can undergo treatment and recuperate in any part of the country for much less than what it would cost them for a treatment in other countries. For example, a normal cardiac bypass surgery (CABG) in Malaysia would cost around US$9,000.

Malaysia offers a wide choice of state-of-the-art private medical centres boasting an impressive array of sophisticated diagnosis, therapeutic and in-patient facilities. These establishments are well-equipped and staffed to ensure the highest level of professionalism, safety and care to patients. Most private medical centres have certifications for internationally recognized quality standards such as MS ISO 9002 or have been given accreditation by the Malaysian Society for Quality of Health.

Most private medical centres in Malaysia also offer comfortable accommodation ranging from private rooms to suites for single occupancy or more. Room charges, inclusive of meals, vary at medical centres but are attractively priced. Some medical centres even provide highly qualified and trained private nurses and personal butlers at a reasonable cost.

In brief, factors that contribute to making Malaysia a centre of medical excellence in the region are listed below:

- Safe and politically stable country
- Wide choice of world class infrastructure facilities e.g. National Heart Institute and Tun Hussein Onn National Eye Hospital
- Competitive and affordable pricing and favourable exchange rate e.g. a normal cardiac bypass surgery would only cost around US$9,000.
- Highly qualified, experienced and skilled consultants with foreign qualifications
- Multi-cultural and religions to accommodate all patients of different cultures and religions
- Communication is easy - English speaking Medical Staff
- State of the Art technology such as MRI, 64-Slice CT Scan, PET Scanner for early detection of cancer and other diseases, cyberknife which is able to radiate tumours without damaging adjacent vital structures
- Quality and safety system in place such as ISO and accreditation by the Malaysian Society for Quality in Health (MSQH)
- Attractive and affordable packages during recuperation period.

To ease entry formalities for patients, the Immigration Department of Malaysia has implements the Green Lane System at main entry points which expedites custom clearance for medical travellers. Accompanying family members or friends of the patient can take advantage of their visit to sample Malaysia's various interesting tourist attractions. Cities like Kuala Lumpur and Penang offer a truly comprehensive range of both health and tourism services, all within easy reach. Penang, for example, is not just home to many hospitals and medical centres; it boasts the rejuvenating air of Penang Hill, the cozy warmth of shady beaches, and endless cultural discoveries.

STATISTICS

Statistics indicate a strong and growing interest in Malaysia's healthcare tourism industry. According to the Association of Private Hospitals Malaysia, the number of foreigners seeking healthcare services in Malaysia has grown from 75,210 patients in year 2001 to 296,687 patients in year 2006 which generated a total of RM203.66 million (USD 59 million) in revenue. In 2007, Malaysia received 341,288 medical tourists with revenue of RM253.84 million.

BRIEF BACKGROUND

Under Malaysia's current health tourism promotion drive, 35 private hospitals in the country have been identified to promote Malaysia as a health tourist destination.

Malaysia's success in establishing itself as a regional hub for excellent healthcare, capable of providing state-of-the-art medical facilities and services for health tourists, began following the setting up of the National Committee for the Promotion of Health Tourism in January 1998.

Besides the Health Ministry, the Committee includes the Ministry of Tourism, the Association of Private Hospitals of Malaysia and other government agencies such as the Malaysian Association of Tours and Travel Agencies, Malaysian Airlines and several private hospitals.

The Committee has been cooperating with other agencies in carrying out promotional activities concerning health tourism in the country. This includes collaborations with the Malaysian External Trade Development Corporation (MATRADE) through its trade missions; Tourism Malaysia through its promotional activities; various state governments; private hospital groups and the Association of Private Hospitals Malaysia.

Medical tourism, numbers in Malaysia are exponentially growing. Medical tourism figures of patients grew from 75, 210 in years 2001 to 296, 678 in year 2006. And this figure of medical tourism patients grew further to 341, 288 in years 2007. The increase in revenue from medical tourism jumped from USD 46 Million approximately in year 2005, 59 Million in year 2006 and 77 Million approximately in year 2007. This growth is expected at rate of about 30% on year on year basis till year 2010, projected by Association of Private Hospitals of Malaysia, APHM.

The healthcare sector and best practices in Malaysia is a very good example of Malaysia's success in providing excellent health care facilities to its general public and medical tourism guests. This is proved through its stringent measures to be ethics based rather business oriented. This is something which is directly related to the outcomes of healthcare provision to patients. We have heard some terrifying stories about a favorite medical tourism destination for Plastic and Cosmetic surgery that patients go for procedures and never come out of hospitals. This is because no restrictions are there to check the practice of provision of medical procedures and healthcare. While this is absolutely opposite in Malaysia. The health Ministry in Malaysia has published 35 hospitals all over Malaysia to be promoted for medical tourism. There is a standardization and accreditation body, with the name of MSQH, to make sure, the standard practiced in Malaysia are according to the best practices in the world. This has also enabled provision of really excellent services to medical tourism related guests in Malaysia.

BIBLIOGRAPHY

- AIIMS claims cutting edge stem cell study-Health/ Sci-The Times of India
- AIIMS pioneers stem cell injection-Delhi-Cities-The Times of India
- André Durand: History of the International Committee of the Red Cross. Volume II: From Sarajevo to Hiroshima. Henry Dunant Institute, Geneva 1984, ISBN 2-88044-009-2
- Stem cell therapy - Hope and scope in pediatric surgery Gupta DK, Sharma S, - J Indian Assoc Pediatr Surg
- Delhi HC stays Venugopal's dismissal; doctors to resume work. The Times of India.
- David P. Forsythe: Humanitarian Politics: The International Committee of the Red Cross. Johns Hopkins University Press, Baltimore 1978, ISBN 0-8018-1983-0.
- Jafari, J. (1974). Creation of the intergovernmental world tourism organization. Annals of Tourism Research, 2, (5), 237–245.
- United Nations General Assembly. (1969). General assembly – twenty fourth session.
- United Nations World Tourism Organization. (2007). About UNWTO.

• Georges Willemin, Roger Heacock: International Organization and the Evolution of World Society. Volume 2: The International Committee of the Red Cross. Martinus Nijhoff Publishers, Boston 1984, ISBN 90-247-3064-3

• Pierre Boissier: History of the International Committee of the Red Cross. Volume I: From Solferino to Tsushima. Henry Dunant Institute, Geneva 1985, ISBN 2-88044-012-2

• International Committee of the Red Cross: Handbook of the International Red Cross and Red Crescent Movement. 13th edition, ICRC, Geneva 1994, ISBN 2-88145-074-1

• John F. Hutchinson: Champions of Charity: War and the Rise of the Red Cross. Westview Press, Boulder 1997, ISBN 0-8133-3367-9.

• UNWTO World Tourism Barometer January 2010. 8. World Tourism Organization. January 2010.

• International Association of Scientific Experts in Tourism. "The AIEST, its character and aims".

• "Recommendations on Tourism Statistics". Statistical Papers. M (New York: United Nations) (83): 5. 1994.

• "UNWTO Tourism Highlights, 2009 Edition". World Tourism Organization. 2009.

• Estimation extrapolated from Paris's tourism office : Key figures

• World Tourism Organization. (2003). WTO news, 2003 (3). Madrid: World Tourism Organization.

• Medical Tourism Consumers in Search of Value 2008 Deloitte Development LLC.

• "CubasMedicalSuccess", BBC News, September 10, 2001.

• Henry Dunant: A Memory of Solferino. ICRC, Geneva 1986, ISBN 2-88145-006-7.

• Jean-Claude Favez, The Red Cross and the Holocaust, Cambridge University Press 1999.

• Angela Bennett: The Geneva Convention: The Hidden Origins of the Red Cross. Sutton Publishing, Gloucestershire 2005, ISBN 0-7509-4147-2.

• David P. Forsythe: The Humanitarians. The International Committee of the Red Cross. Cambridge University Press, Cambridge 2005, ISBN 0-521-61281-0.

• "Healthcare in India". Boston Analytics. http://bostonanalytics.com/india_watch/Healthcare%20in%20India %20Executive%20Summary.pdf.

• "2.5 million people in India living with Aids, according to new estimates". New York Times.

• "2.5 million people in India living with HIV, according to new estimates". World Heath Organization.

• Robinson, Simon (2008-05-01). "India's Medical Emergency". Time.

• "'Hunger critical' in South Asia". BBC. 2006-10-13.

• Using shame to change sanitary habits, Los Angeles Times, 6 September 2007

• "UNWTO technical manual: Collection of Tourism Expenditure Statistics" (PDF). World Tourism Organization. 1995. p. 14.

• "UNWTO World Tourism Barometer June 2009". UNWTO World Tourism Barometer (World Tourism Organization) 7 (2). June 2009.

• UNWTO World Tourism Barometer June 2008. **6.** World Tourism Organization. June 2008.

• "Key Visitor Statistics - 2008". Official website. Visit London. 2010. http://www.visitlondonmediacentre.com/images/uploads/London_-_Key_Visitor_Statistics_2009_-_Factsheet.pdf.

• Bremner, Caroline (10 January 2010). "Trend Watch: Euromonitor International's Top City Destination Ranking". Euromonitor International.

• "Record Year For Tourism Receipts In 2009". Singapore Tourism Board.

• "Cumulative Sameday and Overnight Visitor Arrivals Summary by Country/Territory of Residence - 2009". Official website. Hong Kong Tourism Board.

• In 2009, Total cross-boundary visitors to Hong Kong is 29.5 million. International Visitors (including Short-haul markets, long-haul markets, and Taiwan. Excluding Mainland China and Macau) is 10.95 million. International visitors excluding Taiwan, Mainland China, and Macau is 8.9 million.

• "International Visitors to NYC 2009". Official website. NYC & Company. 2010.

• "Dubai tourist numbers drop 5.7%". eTurboNews. Press Trust of India. 1 February 2010.

• Source: Shanghai Municipal Tourism Administration Commission. Travelmole.com

• "Online Etymology Dictionary: tour".

• "Cox & Kings Website".

• Swine flu prompts EU warning on travel to US. The Guardian. April 28, 2009.

• Cooper, Chris; et al (2005). Tourism: Principles and Practice (3rd ed.). Harlow: Pearson Education. ISBN 027368406X. OCLC 466952897.

• "Long-term Prospects: Tourism 2020 Vision". World Tourism. 2004.

INDEX

J

K

L

M

N

O

P

R

S

T

U

W